Praise for *Motherwhelmed*

It would be an injustice to call Motherwhelmed a book; it is a kaleido-scope. With every turn of the page, an awakening is made that forever alters your view of your sense of self, your truth, and your purpose. As I journeyed through Beth's skillfully crafted prose, I found myself unable to stand by as a passive recipient of her message. I needed to act; I needed to sift; I needed to reconsider—and as a result, I came away lighter, clearer, and stronger. If you yearn to stop inviting guilt, failure, and perfection to sabotage your everyday life and your contribution to the world, step into the kaleidoscope that is Motherwhelmed. Turn the page—wake up, stand up, rise up... and live. The world needs the gift of you. ~**Rachel Macy Stafford, New York Times bestselling author, speaker, and certified special education teacher**

"This is not only a book about motherhood, vulnerability, and the overwhelm of both—it's also a story about giving yourself permission to be the woman you envision yourself to be. The woman you know you are deep in your heart. It's a story about motherhood and love, yes, but it's also one of freedom, too. It's not about losing yourself in motherhood, but finding yourself through it. It's beautiful and life-changing." ~**Colleen Temple, writer + editor of Motherly's *This Is Motherhood***

In a culture where mothers are endlessly bombarded with messages to do more, be more, and give more, Beth's words are a balm for the tired mother's soul. With empathy, compassion, honesty, and grace, Beth meets you where you are, takes your hand, and shows you another way. Instead of shaping you to be worthy of motherhood, she transforms motherhood to be worthy of *you*. Beth offers us a place where mothers can do more than survive: where we all may thrive, if only we take the risk to rethink, relearn, and soar. ~**Rachel Jepson Wolf, Author of** *The Unplugged Family Activity Book* **and** *Herbal Adventures*

A validating, cathartic, and necessary read for every modern mother. *Motherwhelmed* is food for the soul as it brilliantly unpacks the inner and outer barriers to our authenticity and true happiness as over-worked moms. Berry candidly shares her deeply relatable missteps and misgivings as a parent, along with her journey back to herself, giving mothers everywhere an inspiring and do-able blueprint for their own peace, healing, and relief from care-taking overwhelm. Berry also empowers the reader by pointing out our real superpowers as moms - and psssst - it's not "doing it all!" ~**Brandy Ferner, author of** *Adult Conversation: A Novel*

In one of the most relatable books I have ever read, Beth so eloquently and exquisitely puts into words the unique challenges of modern-day motherhood and the narratives we have created about what it means to be a mother. Beth takes us on a journey of exploration and curiosity as she empowers us to reclaim our inherent worthiness and value as mothers. ~**Taylor Kulik, Sleep & Wellbeing Specialist**

MOTHERWHELMED

CHALLENGING NORMS, UNTANGLING TRUTHS, AND RESTORING OUR WORTH TO THE WORLD

BETH BERRY

Revolution from Home Publishing
www.revolutionfromhome.com

Publisher's Cataloging-in-Publication data Berry, Beth.

Editor: Christi McGuire
Cover design: David Wardle
Interior design: Andrea Reider
Author Photograph: Jote Khalsa

ISBN: 978-1-7346717-0-4 (paperback)
ISBN: 978-1-7346717-1-1 (ebook)

1. Motherhood
2. Parenting
3. Women's Empowerment
4. Conscious Parenting

First Edition

"There comes a point where we need to stop just pulling people out of the river. We need to go upstream and find out why they're falling in."

—Desmond Tutu

"If we attempt to act and to do things for others and for the world without deepening our own self-understanding, our own freedom, integrity and capacity to love, we will not have anything to give to others."

—Thomas Merton

"The art of mothering is to teach the art of living to children."

— Elaine Heffner

Dedication

I dedicate this book to my daughters, for awakening me; to Hunter, for believing in me; and to all the mothers and grandmothers—both in the visible and invisible realms—who've remembered, spoken up, broken free, and protected wildness toward my soul's liberation.

CONTENTS

A BOW TO THE SACRED MOTHER

(And a Note from the Author)

W hen I set out to write this book, I figured it would take me three, *maybe* six months to complete. Because I'm at such close range—because I, myself, feel mother-whelmed so much of the time—I assumed that reflecting on motherhood would be a piece of cake. But just as motherhood itself rarely unfolds as we imagine, the reality of writing a book about motherhood, while very much in the depths of mother*ing*, has been nothing like the journey I thought I'd signed up for. Though it would be easy to blame the hundred million needs and interruptions of my four children for the seven *years* it's turned into (okay, I partially blame them), a truer story is this ...

Sometimes I can access clarity in the midst of chaos, and sometimes I can't. Sometimes I have the emotional reserves to deconstruct the messier aspects of my life, and sometimes it's all I can do just to survive them. Sometimes I feel confident in my reflections, and sometimes I feel much too vulnerable and sensitive to share them. And sometimes I feel brave enough to speak my truth, while other days I'd rather play my introvert card and hide.

A while back, another factor in the delay became clear to me: the same perfectionism and passion that defined my early years as a mother showed up in the early years of my writing career. The pressure I put on myself has been immense, and now that I see it, it seems almost laughable.

I was trying to *solve* the problem of motherwhelm, not only for myself but also for the whole of The Mother*hood*. And because there were still so many days when motherhood kicked my butt, my inner critic ran wild, making a real mess of my inner landscape. She said things like, "What makes you an authority on this? Just look how imperfect your own life is!" and "Oh, yeah? You want to write a book called *Motherwhelmed*? Well, let's make sure you're experiencing a heavy dose of it just to keep you humble," and "Sure would be easier to catch up on the laundry, don't you think? Besides, your family needs you. Isn't this project a little on the *selfish* side?"

Thing is, I would recognize that voice anywhere. She was my constant companion while I was raising babies and used to say things to me like, "Nice work cleaning the house and paying the bills. Too bad you practically ignored your kids in order to get it all done," and "Sure, you got dinner on the table, but the girls fought the whole time you ate. What does that say about your priorities?" and "Don't worry, all you have to do is sleep less and sacrifice more and you'll get ahead, eventually."

By recognizing these voices as one in the same, I suddenly had access to all my favorite, well-worn tools for re-centering myself in my truth and power. Here's what I realized once I put them to use:

- It's not a problem that it's taken me six years to finish this book. It's my thoughts about the timeline that have been causing me stress and anxiety.
- Perfection is not a prerequisite for showing up and sharing my heart. If it were, no one would ever share anything, *ever*.
- It is not my job to solve anyone's problems. The solutions to the struggles we're all facing are as diverse and individual as each

and every mother experiencing them. There are plenty of other reasons to write a book.

But the most beautiful realization of all was that motherhood has served as my primary vehicle for growth and transformation. I have both lost and found myself again through motherhood. It has been the backdrop for my heroine's journey.

Given this realization, the answer to "What gives you the authority to write this book?" became clear ... I am not an expert on motherhood; I am a faithful, lifelong student of it. There is no subject on earth I revere more, no humans on earth I respect more, and nothing my heart longs to protect, nourish, restore worth to, shed light on, support the healing of, or advocate for more on this entire planet. I feel for motherhood what I imagine others do for sea turtles or endangered aquifers or old-growth forests. I see the threats to our collective well-being clearly, and cannot, *will not*, pretend them away.

Charles Eisenstein spoke of this idea in a piece he wrote about endangered rhinos:

> I imagine myself talking to a rhino in a cage. She asks me, "What were you doing with your life, while I was going extinct?" If I answer her, "I was working to save the coral reefs," or "I was helping to stop the Navy from using whale-deafening sonar," or "I spent my life trying to free men from death row," then she is satisfied, and so am I. We both know that somehow, all of these endeavors are in service to the rhinos too. I can meet her gaze without shame.[1]

Protecting motherhood and helping to empower mothers are those endeavors for me. It is from this spirit of honor and reverence for The Sacred Mother and her myriad manifestations that I offer you the following perspectives, stories, and truths of my heart.

"Whatever, Mom. You're just motherwhelmed. Chill out."
"OMG, Mom. You're totally motherwhelming me."
"Mom, save your advice for the motherwhelmed."
"That outfit has motherwhelm written all over it."

—My daughters' comments, to me,
over the course of this book's creation.

INTRODUCTION

I'm guessing you didn't haul buckets from a creek this morning. I doubt you skinned a bird or swung an ax or banked coals for your cookfire either. Likely, your babies stayed warm through the night, hunger pains were not the reason you didn't sleep well, and there was no threat to your only food source dragging you out of bed before dawn.

And yet, assuming you're a mother—no matter your age, demographic, convictions, or number of children—you're no stranger to struggle. As far as we've come (in the developed world) from dire conditions as our daily reality, how many mothers do you know whose contentment and inner peace actually *reflect* our relative, recent advantage?

In fact, between your stress level, pace, obligations, car time, guilt, and unending uncertainty, you may even find yourself *longing* for a little house on the prairie—chamber pot, grasshopper plague, and all.

What is going on? Why, considering how far we've come from even our grandmothers' daily realities, does motherhood *still* feel so frustrating?

I spent my first twelve years as a mother asking myself this question in more ways than I care to remember. I'd bet my dream house in Mexico that you've also wondered:

- Why is it that no matter how much I do, buy, make, organize, work, sacrifice, and simplify, I never feel I've done *enough*?
- Will it ever slow down or is this pace just par for the course now that I'm a parent?
- How can I possibly protect their health, well-being, and developing sense of self when it's me against marketers backed by *millions*?
- Am I giving enough of the *right* things to my family, and if so, why am I constantly second-guessing myself?
- Do I really have to be super stressed in order for my family to flourish?
- Is this *really* all there is to my story?

Those first dozen years I was hell-bent on doing things "right." *Right* according to the parenting paradigms that made the most sense to me; *right* according to my countercultural convictions; *right* according to the feeling of magic I hoped to impart from my own childhood; and *right* according to all that my beautiful babies clearly deserved.

Passionate about so many things and wired like the most ferocious of mother mammals, I could see no other way. It was either do things "right" or sacrifice my children's best interests, and what *good* mother would choose the latter?

But the right way didn't deliver. No matter how eco-friendly their lunch boxes, organic our food, sacrificial my spirit, or attached my parenting style, I rarely felt relief from my frustrations. Like laundry and junk mail and car-seat crumbs, my frustrations were always there, reminding me of all I'd yet to accomplish, all the chaos I couldn't seem to calm, and all the goodness I couldn't afford to provide.

I was doing the best I could, yet by the measure of *how I felt*, I was barely passing, even on my best day.

It's been eleven years since I first examined that story. The story that I never do enough. The story that my kids deserve a way of life that means *enduring* my own. The story of *Me Against the Man, The World Is Totally Screwed Up*, and *Mom Is Superhuman*.

This book is about the life I've created and discoveries I've made since then. Since I stopped blaming my (now ex) husband, my culture, and my stage in life for my discontentment and realized that I was the only one responsible for my happiness and fulfillment. Since I quit pretending I was strong and brave and capable enough to go it alone and started admitting I had needs and limitations. Since trading what I was absolutely sure of for what might be possible. Since moving my family to Mexico for four life-changing years abroad.

My daughters are now 13, 15, 19, and 25 years old. I'm still in the thick of it, and expect I'll be here for quite some time. But while challenging as ever, my life no longer feels like a losing battle. My days are no less messy, but my priorities feel much straighter. My kids still fight like mad, but I've learned to quiet my mind. My body never did "bounce back" after babies, but I've moved beyond self-acceptance and into a whole new awareness of what it means to be beautiful. My days are a far cry from efficient, predictable, easy, balanced, or any other trait that our culture claims will bring happiness. But richness and abundance are mine, no matter how bleak the balance in my bank accounts.

What shifted? Amazingly little, aside from my *thoughts*, which have shaped my *stories,* which have changed my *everything*.

In the following chapters, we'll explore the messy frontier of modern-day motherhood we're all attempting to navigate. By sorting social norms and commonly held "truths," getting real about what's working and what's not, and sharing from my personal mothering experience, it is my heartfelt hope that the purpose of this book be realized uniquely and powerfully by awakening mothers from all walks.

The fourfold purpose of this book is:

1. To help you sort your own stories, the true ones from the rest, and let go of those that no longer serve you.
2. To offer a safe, nonjudgmental space within which to consider your truest needs and deepest desires.
3. To honor the uniqueness of your soul and the importance of its expression.
4. To affirm what you already know: that your role as a mother is *way* more valuable, influential, and transformative than our society makes it seem.

To be clear, this is not a book about parenting. I'm not selling sleep solutions, my kids back talk with the best of them, and our college savings is at least as laughable as yours.

This is a book about you, your greatness, and how important it is that you thrive. It's about untangling yourself from the stories keeping you trapped and deconstructing those that you've outgrown. It's about living your best life and thereby giving your children permission to do the same.

Where you are along your mothering journey doesn't matter here. Whether single and 17 (as I was when I started), or 65 and giddy with grandmotherhood, the important thing is that somewhere deep down, you *know* there's more to the story and *feel* life could be better.

I can't pave your path, determine where it will lead you, or lower the speed limit on your life, but I can hold a lantern, and I'd gladly hold your baby if I could.

You are welcome here, however messy your life, heavy your heart, or motherwhelmed you may be.

Chapter 1

ABSORBING THE IMPACT OF CULTURAL DYSFUNCTION

> We all begin the process before we are ready, before we are strong enough, before we know enough; we begin a dialogue with thoughts and feelings that both tickle and thunder within us. We respond before we know how to speak the language, before we know all the answers, and before we know exactly to whom we are speaking.
>
> —CLARISSA PINKOLA ESTÉS

I didn't know what I was signing up for when I decided to become a mother at the age of 16. Milk-soaked sheets and mastitis weren't realities I'd ever considered as I peed on my first pregnancy test stick in the bathroom I shared with my little sisters. Decision fatigue and nervous system overload were still far from my radar as the nurse at Planned Parenthood gently encouraged me to confide in my parents and helped me consider my options. And though only months prior, I'd driven home wasted in the middle of the night, it didn't occur to me that the centimeter-long fetus inside me would one day worry me sick at 2:00 a.m. in many of the same ways I'd recently tortured my own parents.

Today, at age 42, I'm convinced that no mother of any age *really* knows what she's getting into when she agrees to the journey of motherhood. I'm also convinced that this is a saving grace for our species. Who would sign up, knowing the terms of such a contract? Can you imagine?

Contract for Modern-Day Motherhood

I, Beth Berry, agree to an undetermined number of years/decades of sleepless nights, rude comebacks, temper tantrums, chaos management, unending menial tasks, and unrecognized emotional labor. I understand that I will never be paid for this work, that I will rarely be thanked for my efforts, and that I will likely be criticized and judged by family and strangers, alike, no matter how intentionally I invest my time and energy. I also understand that I will be expected to wear multiple hats and fill many roles at once, which will shift constantly and at random, according to the needs of others, including but not limited to: cook, cleaning lady, emotional support manager, household manager, butt wiper, vomit cleaner, wrangler of humans with flailing limbs, tutor, advocate, mediator, playmate, food intolerance expert, best practices researcher, chauffeur, and spiritual guide. I assume all inherent risks of this position, including daily isolation, self-doubt, guilt, anxiety, stress, the minimization/denial of my own needs, and the sometimes-crippling fear that I will fuck things up and scar my babies for life. I understand that though frequent sweetness, love, awe, and laughter are likely, they are not guaranteed and will often be interrupted by fighting, screaming, hitting, threats of self-harm, and/or waves of depression. I accept that I will be given zero on-the-job training and that most of the guidance I receive from this point forward will be conflicting, unsolicited, and ultimately not all that helpful.

Sign here, please. _____

Though a mother's job description has never been particularly sexy, becoming a mother these days is uniquely burdensome. I'd even go so far as to say that we're navigating not only a whole new set of stressors as mothers but also forms of oppression, the likes of which our foremothers never could have imagined (more on that in chapter seven). And while we may not sign actual contracts at the onset of our journey, it often feels as if we have. From the time we even think of having kids, we begin making agreements with ourselves, with those around us, with the world at large, and with whatever spiritual forces we believe in. These largely unconscious agreements can go unexamined for decades—even entire lifetimes—binding us, as if contractually, to ways of thinking and behaving that may or may not be serving us or those we love.

Twelve years ago, utterly overwhelmed, discouraged, and miserable as an all-in, self-sacrificial, stay-at-home mother of four, I decided to rip up my contract. In that sobering moment, which I'll share with you later, there was no dramatic display of paper tearing or animated refusal. Just a quiet, whole-body, rock-bottom knowing that I could not live another minute under the weight of the life I'd created for myself.

I may not have known what I was signing up for when I decided to become a mother, but what I did know—what I could feel deep in my bones—was that I was stepping into a role that was irrefutably important. I knew, even at 16 years old, that I was saying yes to something immensely meaningful and life changing and purposeful and sacred.

A dozen years into the journey, however, my role as a mother didn't feel sacred *in the least*. It felt stifling. It felt draining. It felt utterly and completely overwhelming. And though partly created by me, for the good of those I loved most, it even felt toxic. I didn't know what needed to change, or where those changes would take me, but I did recognize that if I didn't begin to do things differently, my girls would ultimately suffer right alongside me.

My love for my daughters was my primary motivation for learning to love myself.

Let me guess: You signed your mothering contract unconsciously too? It's okay, most of us do. It doesn't matter how naïve we once were or how many messes we created from a less-aware place. What matters is that we begin to see that unconscious contracts can be rewritten. What matters is that we take advantage of this uniquely powerful time within history, when women finally have enough resources and free-dom to shape their lives and choose something better. What matters is that we wake up to our potential as mothers to influence change, to perpetuate cultural healing, and to revive the Sacred Feminine in our hearts, our homes, and our soul-starved world.

The Hardest Hit

Nearly every day, I encounter a mother in the thick of it. Whether she's wrestling her kicking toddler into his car seat while trying not to drop her screaming newborn, enduring the stinging comebacks of her angry teen, spanking her kid in the parking lot when she thought no one was watching, or sharing her sense of inadequacy with me during a session, my heart aches for her. Even when I encounter someone mothering in a way that makes little sense to me, such as allowing a newborn baby to scream himself hoarse in a shopping cart rather than picking him up and soothing him, all it takes is one glance at her despairing or embarrassed or frazzled or hardened expression, and compassion floods my senses. I *feel* her struggle with every maternal inch of my being.

I feel the weight of the million choices she faces and the resulting self-doubt and uncertainty.

I feel the guilt she carries for all she hasn't accomplished and can't provide.

I feel the intense love she holds in her heart and the intense fear right alongside it.

I feel the anxiety she fights and her struggle to keep up with *all the things*.

I feel the shame she endures over her imperfect body, her imperfect parenting, and the moments when she hardly even recognizes herself in the woman she has become.

I feel the exhaustion she copes with while trying to wear so many hats and never feeling she can give anything the attention it deserves.

I haven't always had access to this level of empathy. In fact, I used to feel annoyed and discouraged by mothers who made vastly different decisions than I did. But twenty-five years of motherhood has softened my edges, expanded my awareness, thoroughly kicked my butt, and schooled me hugely in humility. I now see that no matter how different we may be when it comes to our choices, values, and priorities, we're all exactly the same in one essential regard:

We are all trying—as best we can and know how to—to narrow the gaps we feel.

There's nothing mysterious about these gaps. They're exactly what they sound like: distance between one place and another or, in this case, one set of realities and another. Perhaps you can relate with a few of those that I've attempted to narrow in my own life over the years:

- The gap between the holistic education I felt my children deserved and what we could afford to give them.

- The gap between my values and those perpetuated by popular culture.
- The gap between my many passions and the time and energy I've had to pursue them.
- The gap between the chaotic-feeling home we had and the calm, tidy home I dreamed of.
- The gap between the marriage I had and the marriage I longed and strove for.
- The gap between my intuition and what others told me was most important.
- The gap between the wholesome, outdoorsy childhood experiences of old, and the screen-heavy, play-threatened culture of today.
- The gap between the income we needed to live comfortably and my heart's insistence that I stay home with my babies.
- The gap between the stress, overwhelm, and guilt I felt and the peace, connection, and ease with which I longed to be living.
- The gap between all I felt responsible for and what I was actually able to control.

I used to think I was among the struggling few who felt this way, who couldn't seem to get her act together. Years of supporting and bearing witness to the journeys of dozens of friends and hundreds of clients, however, has shown me just how central this theme is in most every mother's life.

Of course, mothers aren't the only ones attempting to close the gaps we feel. All humans share the desire to improve their life circumstances. But the combination of several key factors in our experience as modern mothers is distorting and amplifying our perception of these gaps in huge and hugely affecting ways. This never-before-seen set of factors is creating an atmosphere of confusion, frustration, guilt, hurry, anxiety, shame, and isolation, both within mothers' individual experiences and the collective experience of motherhood we all share.

It's affecting our confidence, our prioritization, our sense of what matters most, our inner peace, our perceptions of one another, and most importantly, our perceptions of *ourselves*.

This combination includes, but is not limited to, the following factors:

- Access to an overwhelming amount of information, both helpful and distractingly useless.
- The millions of distorted messages we receive from marketers and others motivated by the desire to make money.
- Car culture, which has us moving at speeds our hearts, souls, and nervous systems (and our children's hearts, souls, and nervous systems) are evolutionarily unaccustomed to.
- The overall pace of our culture that we're either trying to keep up with or expending energy resisting.
- The fact that "it takes a village," but there are no villages.
- A distorted sense of connection that has us reliant upon virtual and electronic connections to fill our voids for real, meaningful, everyday relationships and support.
- A near-constant state of overwhelm due to a drastic increase in the number of options we have and decisions that need to be made (aka decision fatigue).
- Convenience dependence, which inherently means less interaction with people and encourages an even faster pace.
- Huge shifts within the world of parenting regarding what's deemed healthy and acceptable when it comes to interaction and discipline.
- Distractions everywhere we turn.
- The message that pain is something to be avoided at all costs.
- The rampant illusion that perfection is possible.
- The prominence and addictiveness of technology, which affects adults and children alike.

- The fact that most of us are out of touch with our cyclical nature and our interconnectedness with the natural world.
- Our ambivalence when it comes to child-rearing vs. career development.

Though the majority of these factors are affecting all of us, not just mothers, we feel these changes more acutely than most for the following reasons:

- We are biologically wired to protect our children from anything we perceive as a threat (i.e., much of the list above).
- We are inherently more vulnerable and dependent on others during certain seasons of our lives (i.e., postpartum, while raising young children, when navigating the complexities of balancing work for pay with child-rearing and homemaking).
- We're emotionally sensitive creatures by nature, and our emotions shift greatly, depending on hormonal factors and natural cycles.
- Our needs are unique and largely misunderstood, and we often feel ashamed for having needs in the first place.
- We're the first responders. We're the ones experiencing, first-hand, the effects of all this change on the next generation.
- We're natural community builders, but most communities aren't structured in such a way that allows us to do what we're wired for practically, easily, or effectively.
- We're forced to build community ourselves during times of our lives when we need it most but have the least time and energy to do so.

Mothers today are struggling. Not because we're inadequate or weak, but because we're the ones being hardest hit by everything that's changing. We're also some of the least supported, most isolated, and most heavily marketed to among all segments of the population.

Looking back on my own mothering experience, and the rather extreme choices I've made at times, it's clear to me that making everything I could from scratch, justifying a private school we couldn't afford, sewing costumes until two in the morning, running all over town for practices and lessons, overcommitting myself to the point of resentment, and researching grad schools during naptime were all attempts at narrowing these gaps.

On the days when I felt the most overwhelmed and defeated, I was feeling the gaps more acutely and discouraged by my seeming inability to bridge them. When I was feeling particularly good about things, it was because I'd either managed to narrow some of the more significant gaps I was currently experiencing or their intensity had lessened, however temporarily.

Though their variations and manifestations are endless, gaps are quite easy to identify. Simply follow your frustrations.

- When you clean all day only to have your efforts sabotaged within minutes once the kids come home, you're likely feeling a gap between your hard work and the sense of satisfaction and appreciation you crave following a job well done.
- During rush-hour traffic while he screams of "starvation" and she threatens to pee her pants, you're probably feeling a gap between the pace that you're trying to keep up with and a pace that would feel healthier for your family.
- When you receive a note from your child's teacher stating that all snacks to be shared with the class must now be prepackaged because homemade food is no longer allowed, you're likely feeling a gap between your values and the values of our decreasingly nourishing and wholesome culture.
- When your tween begs for a cell phone (again) and your teen ignores you while texting, chances are, you're feeling the gap

between what's ideal for their development and the social norms of their rapidly-changing reality.

- While complained to, ordered to make food, and smeared with snot, simultaneously, perhaps you're feeling a gap between the break you need and the likelihood of you actually getting one.

- When forced to choose, once again, between the happiness of your child and the favor of your boss, you're probably feeling the gap between your desire to be present for your family and your need to provide an income.

- When your work for pay piles up in direct proportion to the stomach flu-soiled laundry, you're likely longing to fill the gap between the support you have and support you dream of.

- When you try on your swimsuit, find the state of affairs to be worse than you thought, and feel crappy for the rest of the day, you're no doubt feeling the gap between what society says you should look like and the reality of postpartum bodies.

- When overdraft charges cause your partner to question, yet again, whether staying home with your baby is really worth it, you're probably feeling the gut-wrenching gap between your partner's need for stability and empathy and your baby's needs for connection and security.

- When you hear of the latest humanitarian or environmental crisis and realize that, though you care deeply, you're too busy at home to make any real difference, you may be beating yourself up over the gap between the impact you want to make and what you currently feel capable of.

Viewed through the lens of frustration, it's easy to see how prevalent our gaps really are. In fact, whatever life dishes out on any given day, frustration is generally served on the side. As common to motherhood as laundry and diapers and shotgun wars, we hardly even question frustration's presence. "Of course we get frustrated," we reason.

"Life is frustrating." We then go about trying to alleviate its intensity in all the ways we've been taught will help us feel better.

We clean, complain, mope, yell, retreat, shop, and scroll through social media. Or, on the days we're a little more in-tuned with what's good for us, we nap, seek empathy, do yoga, go for a run, engage our hobbies, or connect with our partners. The bottom line is that when frustration sets in, *we want to close the gap as quickly as possible*, and when we can't, we engage in all kinds of behaviors to lighten its weighty presence:

We plan the perfect party to make up for our not-so-perfect parenting.

We search for a nicer house with a bigger porch and room for a garden.

We escape to Target where things are tidy, no one's screaming, and we can't see the dirty dishes.

We research alternative schools, Google behavioral disorders, and commiserate with those who share similar struggles.

And of course, when none of that works (or as a first resort, depending on the day), we bust out our chocolate/potato chip/libation of choice.

I lived this way for years, and *sometimes* it seemed to work (meaning that I felt a temporary sense of relief and ease). But as soon as I'd conquer the laundry mountain, we'd be hit with a stomach bug. As soon as we'd pay off a set of braces, the transmission or A/C would go out. And as soon as one girl seemed to be outgrowing her tendency to cry at the drop of a hair tie, another would develop a habit of interrupting or refusing to eat because she felt fat. The more aware I became of all I "could" or "should" be doing to alleviate my problems and theirs alike, the more frustration I felt.

Caught in a self-perpetuating cycle with no lasting solution in sight, I felt stuck, discouraged, and behind most of the time. I hardly recognized myself anymore through my resentment, fatigue, and stress, and I certainly didn't like the woman I was becoming.

What bothered me most, however, was that it was becoming harder to find enjoyment in the day-to-day with my girls. Once, probably toward the end of the day, when I had nothing left to give and my frustrations were too many to hide, my sweet, empathetic 5-year-old looked at me with soft-eyed concern and asked, "Mama, do you like being my mom?"

It broke my heart that she had to ask, that she wasn't sure. My frustrations were no longer mere irritations for me to manage. They were causing my children—the same ones I was working so hard to provide a rich and wholesome life for—to question my enjoyment *of them*.

Clearly, something had to give. I just had no idea *what*.

Chapter 2

THE BATTLE WITHIN

The willingness to rebel from the expected norms, rules, and
silent contracts of establishment comes out of knowing that one
cannot afford to build resentment. Resentment, which comes
from the decision to go against one's truth, embitters the self.
It somaticizes in the body and takes on the burden of pain as
if it were ours alone. The whistleblower, on the other hand,
reveals a shared complicity. It says, "I expect more from myself
and from you." And in that stance, the pain becomes, in a sense,
communal.

—TOKO-PA TURNER

Though I felt painfully alone in my frustrations at the time, I
now know that frequent frustration is a common denomina-
tor among modern-day mothers. Unfortunately, struggling to
enjoy the day-to-day is also a common theme.

A while back—curious about just how universal our experiences are—I asked my blog readers to describe some of *their* frustrations as mothers. Here are some of their responses:

Liz—My kids are 2 and 6. I would love to provide them with an alternative school experience but find the schools with philosophies I like the most to be too expensive. I have been unhappy with the focus on drilling my son on sight words and letter sounds in public kindergarten. I wish he had more time for exploratory, inquiry-based study, with more focus on play.

Julie—I have two girls, ages 3 and 5. As a stay-at-home mom, I am generally frustrated with trying to balance household management and child-rearing and feeling like I'm not "rockin'" either one. Every day I feel defeated and outnumbered. Add in the balance of time for my marriage, friendships, family, little side jobs and obligations that I have signed up for (attempting to still have "something that's just mine"), sleep, and self-care, and I don't have a clue. I feel like I am bad at life. I see others who have the same on their plates, but they seem to be good at it.

Miranda—I am so frustrated with the lack of adequate paid leave for mothers in this country! Our country cares so little about our children who need their families when they are little. I'm also disgusted with the lack of support for breastfeeding. Ever tried pumping in a corner of a retail pharmacy sitting on a step stool? (I have ... ridiculous.) I'm frustrated with my inability to take care of myself for fear of the guilt of not giving my all to my family 100 percent of the time.

Erika—I have a constant fear that I have not given my children the right tools for their "tool box." Will they be able to make the best choices, stand up for what they know and feel is right, not cave to peer pressure, and remember to look before crossing the street? I cannot impress upon them enough that although they should enjoy playing and exploring our world, they should also be mindful of the possible dangers/accidents/not-so-nice folks that are everywhere. More importantly, I would hope they can execute their lives in a manner that does not (indirectly) make them neurotic! They need to be kind, understanding ... to find balance among the chaos, not to be bullied nor be a bully.

Heather—Right now my main frustration is feeling like I'm not contributing much to the good of the world. I realize it is sort of insane to say when I am doing my best to pour love, purpose, education, nutrition, and values into three whole people! I homeschool and am at the will of their (and my busy husband's) schedules. I am doing exactly what I want to be doing, and yet ...

Annie—I'm 34 years old, and I have two daughters, ages 6 and 3. After much deliberation, I think my biggest frustration as a mother is threefold: self-doubt, guilt, and anger. All three of these nag at me every day. Some days are worse than others. I feel like each day is a battle with myself. I have the good angel on one side whispering into my ear that I have beautiful, smart, loving, fun, active, well-behaved girls and that I am a great mama. Then there is the bad angel on the other side, yelling into my ear about every little obnoxious thing my children do, and my filthy house, and that huge pile of dirty laundry, and that huge pile of clean laundry, and that song I need to work on for that one piano student, and those beanbags I said I would sew for my big girl's kindergarten classroom that I haven't gotten to yet, and that meal I need to cook, and those dishes I need to do, and the animals I need to feed, and the eggs I need to collect, and that friend that I need to call back, and that playdate I need to "regretfully" decline, and, and, and, and! And I am a complete failure as a human being, not to mention mother!

And then I snap ... yelling and screaming ensues. It comes out of my mouth, and I instantly regret it. I am filled with guilt and self-loathing and regret. It is insanely frustrating to feel this way! And then some days I remember. I remember to say, "Sure!" Pour myself a glass of wine.

Take a seat in the middle of my piles of laundry. Grab my knitting. Sit back and reflect on my beautiful, messy, vibrant family. Sometimes, when I stop to look, I see how good my life really is.

Octavia—I used to feel so confident in the way I parent and it seems now with so much information, I trust myself less and feel as if I have no idea what I am doing. And it is absolutely untrue.

Juli—I am 36 and mother to two girls, ages 4 and one-and-a-half. I find that there are many parenting challenges, and they change almost daily. The amount of money and prep time it takes to feed my family well is sometimes incredibly trying and tiring. I feel like I cook or clean up from cooking all day sometimes. And that does not even include gardening time during the growing season, bread baking, food preservation, etc. And then all their friends are just fed total junk, and they look at me like I am denying my kids the American way because I do not let them eat processed junk all the time. It is hard to stay strong and not just give in and give them the darn cookie!

I also think one of the biggest challenges facing all mothers in this modern world is too much information. It is hard to feel self-confident in your parenting when there are all these different views and opinions at your fingertips. It can feel very confusing and judgmental at times. It is very easy to start feeling like everyone else knows what they are doing and they are doing it better. And it can make it hard to find your own groove as a parent, because you are so busy Googling what everyone else is doing. It is a tough environment for following your instincts.

My other very large frustration is education. I do not want to send my girls to public school to learn how to obey and memorize. I think there are some major problems in our educational system. Unfortunately, the private options are way out of our price range. I want to homeschool, but I constantly question if I am able to pull that off and if it is in the best interest of my girls. Especially my oldest, who is highly extroverted in an introverted family.

Sarah—I'm 36, mom to 5- and 8-year-old boys. My biggest frustration is never feeling like I've got it all "together." Somehow, someone is always late, forgotten their homework, unbathed, still in yesterday's clothes, eating junk food, or acting like a lawless hooligan. And I am not exempt from the list. I guess I always thought I'd have things figured out by now, rather than constantly struggling to balance my needs, career, household, marriage, and parenting. I never feel like I'm doing well. I do well enough at a few things for a while as the others suffer, then juggle things around to do well enough at a few others. How and when do things ever get balanced and "together"? Oops—ten mommy minutes online and there is chaos in the boys' room. Off I go!

Ashley—I'm a 29-year-old mom to a 7-month-old little boy. My biggest frustration now is the lack of support for families in our society. Sadly, we don't live near family (we are hoping to move closer soon), and it is tough to find a good community that can support us and our son. We have found some, but it is hard. I want my son to be part of a village of people who will hold him and care for him and love on him—and likewise that we can do the same for others. It is just not part of the way we live in this country. My husband and I have talked about trying to house share or do some co-op living, but that's hard to find. Seems very against-the-grain. I work full time and my husband is at home with baby, and it just feels like it would be so much easier (and better for us all) if there was a better way to share the load and the experience with others.

Whether you found yourself nodding in agreement, judging them for what you perceive to be lesser frustrations than your own, or wishing you could hug them and commiserate over tea, you can no doubt empathize with their sense of struggle.

For all our differences, frustration unites modern-day mothers. What, aside from the love we feel for our children, do we feel more often than this?

Consider the short of what they shared:

- Liz knows what she wants for her children but can't afford to provide it.
- Julie feels she's spread so thin she can hardly do anything well.
- Miranda feels that our culture as a whole is unsupportive toward motherhood.
- Erika fears she's not giving her children what they will ultimately need to thrive.
- Heather doubts that her impact in the world is enough.
- Annie wonders if her successes are enough to compensate for her shortcomings.
- Octavia craves certainty in the face of so much information.
- Juli does many things "right," yet feels she's constantly paddling upstream.
- Sarah's always a few steps behind the pace she feels she ought to be keeping up with.
- Ashley longs for a tribe and grieves our culture's lack of community.

Notice a common thread? Annie summed it up succinctly when she said, "I feel like each day is a battle with myself."

She's right. There *is* a battle going on inside most of us: between what we most deeply desire and what appears to be possible; between the way we currently feel and the way we hope to feel when our lives are all lined up; between what's clearly best and what is realistic; and between our busy, logical minds and hurting, heavy hearts.

This gap—the valley in between the lives we have and the lives we deeply desire—is fertile ground for frustration. Fear, worry, anxiety, resentment, confusion, anger, and self-doubt also thrive in this busy valley, and no amount of Googling, house organizing, or high-dollar tutoring can turn our inner battle grounds into peaceful pastures.

A few months ago, while rummaging through a box I hadn't opened in a while, I came across several old DVDs labeled with enough of the right words to make me stop what I was doing and shift gears. "Eli's Entrance" and "Young Estella," had my kids curious, too, and soon, we were all on the couch, eager for a feel-good moment and hoping the DVD player still worked.

The discs' contents weren't all that impressive, actually—a few dozen blurry photos of the girls, messy, everyday moments in the life of our family twelve years ago, and several dizzying videos that had clearly been recorded by young children—but I was moved to tears, nonetheless. While my girls' sweet baby faces made me sigh with nostalgic longing, it was my own exhausted, defeated expressions that really got me. Reminded of just how beat down I felt at the time, my heart ached for the woman I once was. I hadn't merely been frustrated during those years, but *tortured* by the gaps I felt, as each one represented a perceived personal inadequacy.

Seeing my younger self—so determined, so overworked, so spent—filled me with compassion for this person I'd once been so hard on. I was actually *mean* to her at times, my expectations so high that no one in the world could have met them, much less an exhausted, postpartum mother of four.

Allow me to paint a picture of those crazy-beautiful days, when my gaps seemed to be growing even more quickly than my girls.

Chapter 3

MY EARLY DAYS
AS A MOTHER

We are constantly trying to hold it all together. If you really want to see why you do things, then don't do them and see what happens.

—MICHAEL A. SINGER

The path to a better tomorrow was crystal clear to me in my early 20s. It looked like environmental stewardship, utter dedication to the causes in line with my (many) convictions, the noble deferment of pleasures, and the optimistic pursuit of sustainability. Already a mother of two by age 22, intentional domesticity was the way in which I intended to change the world. Practically speaking, that meant diapers hung to dry, clothes handmade and repurposed, organic food or be damned (I assumed), alternative schools whatever the cost, and a baby on my boob, back, or bed at all times.

I adored my baby girls. They were my everything, and motherhood suited me well.

I felt pretty good about the impact we were making (or not making, as it were) until our third daughter was born. Even on the more challenging days, I managed to keep reality at bay by beating it back with daily doses of *idealism*. Kids not cooperating? No problem. We'd shift gears and craft the day away. Pink eye running through the family? Thank God for breastmilk. Frustrated by the state of the world? I'd get busy digging garden beds.

Assuming righteous living to be The Way to inner fulfillment, I set my sights on what seemed best and worked as hard as I could to meet every goal I set for myself, however lofty or seemingly insane.

By the time we were 25 and 24, respectively, Hunter and I had wet our feet in many a passion. We'd managed an organic, free-range poultry operation on a 1,200-acre ranch, spearheaded biointensive market gardens at a local health food store, lived in and learned to build the most sustainable homes on the planet (we're still Earthship junkies), bought the cheapest land we could find, and eventually made home in a 220-square foot tool shed because ... sacrifice and sustainability! (Also, we were broke, brave, and youthfully optimistic.)

On a rainy Texas day in December, having recently scored a truck bed full of fence pickets and repurposed them into a porch kitchen, we were cooking dinner in coats and hats when I announced that not four, but five of us would soon be sharing our one-room abode.

Channeling the misfortune-turned-fortitude of my foremothers, I roughed it through that pregnancy willingly. Thinking hot water showers and indoor plumbing was the very *least* we could sacrifice toward the salvation of the species, I held onto the hope that with just a *little* more dedication and making do and just a *few* more years of sweat equity, we might actually begin to feel like we were making a real difference. Another rainwater barrel and garden bed or two and my soul might finally find solace from the heavy realization slowly descending upon us:

No matter how much we did, it would never be enough.

Daughter number three was born in that tool shed. Her first bath was in the shade of a tree-canopied sink we'd recently salvaged.

A rather concerned and more conventionally-minded friend brought us a Costco-sized package of Styrofoam plates when she came to visit after the birth. I cried as much from relief as defeat and hormones and used them gratefully ... but guiltily.

Once we'd finished building the "Big House" (an 800-square foot cabin) and following three years of commuting forty minutes one way for The Only Shot My Eldest Had at a Healthy Childhood (I mean, a Waldorf School), we gave up the homesteading dream (temporarily), moved to town (the commute was killing us) and (surprise!) got pregnant again. Apparently, lemon water has a higher success rate as a contraception when you're not so exhausted by the rest of your naturally-planned family that you fall asleep without actually *using* it.

I hardly remember that next year of baby-soaked survival mode. Reality had finally found me and was apparently pissed that I'd managed to evade it for so long. Totally at random, it would sneak up on me, and before I even knew what was happening, I'd do totally crazy things like toss a bag of disposable diapers in the grocery cart or stock up on frozen pizzas. Then, in an attempt to hide again, I'd go home and sew prairie dresses or bake bread or plan the most wholesome pumpkin-themed party ever, lest my children's memories be forever tainted by their mother's utter and obvious weakness of spirit.

Utterly perplexed over our choices, my sister-in-law once asked me, "Don't you ever just dream of the *easy* life? Don't you sometimes just want to watch movies and eat junk food and not care so much about making a difference?" My desperate-to-dispel-her-doubts-about-my-dedication response? "Nope. No way. How will the state of the world ever improve if those of us willing to *be the change* give up?"

Like reality, my tipping point came quite without warning. While nursing newborn number four on our toddler-tainted hand-me-down couch, sandwiched between my fighting two- and 6-year-olds, and being screamed at about the state of our messy (940-square foot) home by my freshly-adolescent firstborn, I realized that while I adored my children and was clearly blessed beyond measure, I hated my life.

Between cleaning classrooms to pay for The Ideal School (with a baby on my back and a toddler underfoot), homeschooling the next in line because I could only clean so much, tandem nursing to meet the needs of both babies, raising ducks in our tiny backyard because I couldn't let go of the homesteading dream *completely*, buying organic food even when we were broke (and beating myself up when I couldn't), still hanging diapers as often as I could just to keep the sustainability gods from striking me dead, and completely resenting my husband for, oh, just about everything, I had sacrificed everything in me to be the best human and mom I could be. And even so, I had "failed."

It was either compromise (the dreaded *C* word) or lose my maternal mind.

Yes, we were young, and no, not everyone is nearly so extreme in their passion pursuits, but we really, truly thought we were doing what was best. We were disciplined. We were committed. We were willing to make sacrifices. We had the hearts of *changemakers*.

Looking back, I realize that while my intentions were pure and rooted in love, there is a big difference between *being the change* and *being the bridge*. Ghandi didn't say, "Work yourself to death in order to create the change you wish to see," or "Lay yourself down in the space between two realities and let yourself be trampled for the greater good." He said, "*Be* the change you wish to see in the world." But doing so would have required that I extend the same love, passion, and compassion I felt toward my family and the environment to *myself*, and who had time for such a thing with so much work to be done in the world? Besides, I clearly wasn't worthy of such loving kindness. Look how far behind I was in every aspect of my life!

The Unsustainability of Self-Sacrifice

Self-sacrifice as a way of life is not uncommon among mothers. Biologically wired to protect and nurture, we naturally give of ourselves in our children's seeming best interests. But this evolutionary miracle isn't mixing too well with current cultural norms. The combination of our love, hormones, the dozens of gaps we feel, and the millions of choices we have to make is thoroughly messing with our heads and hearts. The result is an entire generation of mothers who feel responsible for building the bridges, buying the bridges, or *being* the bridges between each of these gaps, in order to qualify as "good mothers." This ends up looking like many different things:

- We say "yes" to more when we're already maxed.
- We go to great lengths in order to idealize our children's life experiences and minimize their pain.
- We spend money we really don't have (and on things we may not need).
- We research solutions incessantly and constantly wonder what we're doing wrong.
- We deplete our reserves of energy, taking little to no time for ourselves.
- We feel guilty and behind most of the time.
- We form a sense of self based on our ability or inability to close the gaps we perceive as most important.
- We lose touch with the essence of who we are in order to support and protect our *children's* treasured essence.

Oftentimes, it's the more intentional, invested mothers among us who suffer most from this mind-set. Not only are we committed to what's "best" for our children (and the planet and humanity), but many of us are willing to forgo comforts and conveniences, even sacrifice our own well-being for the sake of a better world. As I learned the hard way, however, self-sacrifice as a lifestyle isn't sustainable. Eventually, it leads to resentment, burnout, a perception of even more gaps in need of filling, and an unkind, distorted sense of self.

Decreased self-esteem and self-worth aren't the only consequences of our unexamined gap-closing obsessions. This phenomenon is affecting nearly every aspect of our lives:

- When people don't see our gaps as we do, we often become defensive and feel even more isolated in our struggles.
- When other mothers prioritize different gaps than we do, we become divisive and feel threatened by one another.
- Our children become dependent on us as their gap-fillers and begin to see that they have the power to illuminate and manipulate gaps in order to have their desires fulfilled.
- Big businesses become even more powerful as they study, cater to, and profit from our unmet needs, fears, and frustrations.
- Our sense of freedom is compromised as we spend the majority of our time and energy fulfilling perceived obligations and trying to "keep up" rather than creating our lives based on the truth, beauty, and uniqueness of who we are and why we're here.

Here's the thing, though ... we're often reacting not to actual inadequacies or problems but to unchecked, oppressive stories we've bought into or created regarding our responsibilities, our children's needs, and our culture's inherently destructive influence on their lives. The reason so many of our gap-narrowing strategies don't work (or don't work for long) is that they address mere symptoms but rarely the root causes of the gaps we're feeling. Like slapping a Band-Aid on a broken bone, true healing simply can't happen until we dig beneath the problems we initially perceive (which are often created by and lining the pockets of profiteers) and address the subcutaneous craters we're actually feeling.

We're not only frustrated because we can't get our kid to buckle into his car seat quickly enough. We're also frustrated because our culture encourages a pace that is clearly not in the best interest of our families and we can't figure out what to do about it.

We're not only frustrated because our teenager mouthed off yet again but also because he's disconnecting from us and we're terrified of losing him.

We're not only frustrated because our baby won't sleep through the night but also because somewhere along the way, we decided she should.

We're not only frustrated because our kids are fed junk food, images, and ideas day in and day out but also because those influences are amplified by billions of dollars, making our voices seem washed out and insignificant.

Narrowing the gaps (as opposed to denying them, busying ourselves so we don't feel them as deeply, beating ourselves up for their existence, or filling them with comforts and distractions), requires an honest look at how they got there in the first place. It requires that we understand who stands to gain by ensuring that our gaps stay wide and plentiful. It requires challenging cultural norms, waking up to a new way of looking at the world, opening our hearts even when it hurts, and most importantly, healing our relationships with ourselves. It requires that we feel good, strong, and connected to who we really are, not merely the idea of who we should be.

Closing the gaps begins with awakening to our stories.

Chapter 4

AWAKENING TO OUR STORIES

There's always a story. It's all stories, really. The sun coming up every day is a story. Everything's got a story in it. Change the story, change the world.

—Terry Pratchett

Consider the tone of some of the more popular stories currently being perpetuated within the world of motherhood:

- I should be doing more.
- I should be *accomplishing* more.
- I should have lost my baby weight by now.
- There's never enough time to get it all done.
- I need more ___ or less ___ in order to be happy.
- My house isn't clean/tidy/efficient enough.
- I can't seem to find balance.
- My kids shouldn't be so annoying or act so entitled.

- I'm so far behind.
- I should be making more money.
- I really ought to play with them more.
- She's obviously a better mother than I am.

Depending on your current life circumstances and mind-set, these may not sound like stories to you but absolute truths. You may be looking around your messy house thinking, "Uh, it's *obviously* true that I'm behind," or reflecting on your recent experience bathing-suit shopping and feeling utterly disheartened by your "unsightly" figure.

But these ideas came from somewhere. Somewhere along the line you bought into the idea that when the house is messy, it means that you are falling behind. At some point, you adopted the story that your body was supposed to look a certain way in order to be considered adequate, attractive, and lovable.

When you think, "I'm so far behind," how do you feel? Do you feel inspired by your home and life circumstances? Do you feel grateful for the richness and abundance your messy house represents? Do you feel excited to hop up and "get ahead"? More likely, you feel guilty, ashamed, and anxious that someone may show up unexpectedly and see what a mess your life is.

When you think, "I should have lost more weight by now," how do you feel? Are you proud of the miracle of life-creation that took place within your body? Are you grateful for the way your body nurtured your baby, managed to heal, and functions without you having to remind it to breathe, digest, and renew itself, every moment of every day? More likely, you feel shame, embarrassment, inadequacy, and even self-loathing every time you look in the mirror.

However true they may sound, these everyday thoughts and associated emotions are nothing more than culturally conditioned and condoned reactions to popular, normalized stories. Our beliefs that our houses should stay tidy and that our waistlines should be thin aren't based on truth but a set of stories we've been told, sold, and affected by from the time we were born.

Where did these stories come from? Who created them? Most importantly, how are they contributing to or detracting from the quality of our lives?

Is It True?

Until a dozen years ago, at the lowest point in my life, stories weren't something I gave much thought to. Sure, my parents read to me as a young girl, and I've always devoured good books when they've crossed my path. But it wasn't until I considered the following question that the significance, power, and potential *impact* of stories began to sink in: "Who would you be *without* your story?"

Loving What Is was one of "those" books for me. (You know, the life-transforming type that arrives exactly when you need it most.) In it, Byron Katie encourages her readers to examine their thoughts for truth before *creating* their stories, a concept I had never before considered.

"A thought is harmless unless we believe it," she says. "It's not our thoughts, but our *attachment* to our thoughts, that causes suffering. Attaching to a thought means believing that it's true, without inquiring. A belief is a thought that we've been attaching to, often for years."[2] She continues, "Whenever you mentally oppose what is, you're going to experience sadness and apparent separation. There's no sadness without a story."[3]

No sadness without a story? Could this also mean that there's no anxiety, disappointment, or resentment without a story? It seemed too lofty a claim to be true, but I was rather a mess at the time and other elements of her message really resonated, so I kept reading. Hopeful and quite desperate for change, I soon began checking uncomfortable thoughts left and right:

"Is it *true* that I can't feel settled until the house is clean and the bills are paid?"

"Is it *true* that our kids' bank-breaking private school is the only viable option?"

"Is it *true* that her birthday party needs to be even better than last year's, never mind that I have a newborn?"

"Is it *true* that grad school (on top of everything else) will satiate this inexplicable longing I can't seem to shake?"

One by one, I put my stories to the test and, one by one, they proved weak, at best. I was onto something important. I could feel it in my bones.

Driven by what I now recognize as soul starvation, my curiosity grew like a well-watered weed. Who was this story-less me? Might she be happier? More patient? Less frustrated, lonely, and anxious? Little did I know, I had just embarked on a journey of self-discovery and personal growth that would forever alter the course of my life.

Changing My Story

The beginning of that journey was uncomfortable, stressful, and messy, at best. We were living in Austin, TX, which had, by that point, already become the traffic nightmare it continues to be. My days consisted of driving my daughters to four different schools, nursing toddler #4 and part-time homeschooling daughter #3, substitute teaching at the Waldorf school my eldest daughter was attending, teaching fiber arts classes from my home, designing and creating whimsical children's clothing, dolls, and toys to sell at festivals and boutiques, and strategizing ways to save my seriously struggling marriage. It all felt like *so much*, yet I still couldn't figure out what to add, subtract, or multiply in order to slow the pace, catch up, or catch my breath.

The shifts were super subtle at first. I finished Katie's book and started another from the self-help shelves. A friend invited me to attend an Al-Anon meeting with her. I scheduled a massage for myself, even though we didn't have the money for it.

Within months of reading Katie's book, and freed from just enough stories to brave the leap, our family followed a longtime dream and moved to Mexico, where the real discovery soon began. Stepping out of my society's stories, immersed in a whole new way of being, and vulnerable like never before (my daughters and I spoke zero Spanish when we first arrived), every story I'd ever told, been told, or believed since birth was thrown into a Maya soup pot, stirred by toothless abuelitas, and fed to me in heavy doses of humility (to kill the parasites, of course). For four years, I lost myself in meat markets, heartache, and confusing conversations. I breathed smoke from cookfires and sighs of relief that, unlike children born Maya, my babies' lungs were spared the constant coating of tar that lined shack walls and respiratory tracts alike. My intelligence mattered less than my intuition, courage proved more useful than certainty, and the walls I'd built around my heart over a lifetime proved utterly useless in the (smiling) face of abject poverty.

Deeper questions began to rise to the surface. The world as I knew it was falling apart one examined story at a time:

Is it true that the third world needs us to "save" them?

Is it true that affluence breeds happiness?

Is it true that I don't deserve joy until I've done enough things "right"?

Is it true that building walls around my heart will keep me from getting hurt?

Is it true that pain is something to be avoided?

Is it true that *they're* oppressed and *I'm* free?

With every examined thought came a greater opening to the world of possibility. Nothing seemed absolute anymore. It was terrifying, it was thrilling, and I'd never felt more alive.

In the years since it first occurred to me that my thoughts *could* be examined, I've checked hundreds, maybe even thousands, of stories around and within me. Stories told to me by the media, well-meaning friends, and the "experts" about what's most important. Stories I've believed since the time I could talk. Stories about beauty, success, fear, pain, love, and my own worthiness. Stories universal to the human experience, specific to cultures of affluence, and unique to those whose children may or may not ever learn to read.

Of course, I've paid particular attention through the years to the stories in circulation regarding motherhood, both as a mainstay and pertaining to my personal experience. The more deeply I've dug within these stories, particularly those hidden within my own heart, the more clear I am on one thing ...

We're not struggling because we're inadequate, because there's not enough time, or because child-rearing standards have risen. We're struggling because the vast majority of the stories we're being told, adopting, making up, and forming our belief systems around are at least partially untrue, and untrue stories make for lousy foundations when it comes to building a life we love.

The Stories We Adopt

During those early days of motherhood, I was sabotaged daily by stories in and around me. Not all stories, mind you (I've always been leery of the more mainstream ones), but those that stirred my many passions.

I would hear a story (often in the form of a cause I believed in), feel its importance at my core, and feel responsible to alleviate at least some part of its problem. "You're either part of the problem or part of the solution," was my mantra, and I was not about to merely straddle the line.

Problem was, my passions were *endless*. From dying folk arts and watershed protection to breastfeeding and homesteading to personal wellness and food justice, dozens of good and righteous storytellers crowded my thoughts, competed for my energy, and fought for my allegiance.

"Conserve water!"

"Make it from scratch!"

"Teach them to sew!"

"Take them hiking!"

"Shop local!"

"Sacrifice for private school!"

"Do more yoga!"

"Support organic farmers!"

"Feed the starving children!"

Each told a story that resonated with me. Each felt undoubtedly *important*. And so, from a place of pure intentions, I *adopted* those stories like hungry, abandoned babies and allowed them direct access to my internal navigation center.

Like a well-trained dog intent on pleasing her master, I listened and responded to those voices best I could. But with each sacrifice in the name of righteousness, and with each action motivated by the slave driver within me, I felt slightly less empowered and even more overwhelmed.

It seemed my heart for goodness and justice was working *against* me.

Looking back, I realize that I was experiencing what Michael Singer describes so beautifully in his bestseller, *The Untethered Soul*: "If you can't get the world the way you like it, you internally verbalize it, judge it, complain about it, and decide what to do about it. This makes you feel more empowered ... In the thought world, there's always something you can do to control the experience."[4]

But this perceived control of the outer world through exhausting effort, incessant mental chatter, and endless guilt proved worthless toward the joy, peace of mind, and sense of accomplishment I sought.

In fact, the more deeply entrenched I became in my pursuits of passion, the more ineffective I felt in creating the kind of change I so desperately desired.

"In the name of attempting to hold the world together," Singer says, "you're really just trying to hold yourself together ... You have given your mind an impossible task by asking it to manipulate the world in order to fix your personal inner problems."[5]

I had adopted the incredibly powerful story that my *inadequacies* were the reason I couldn't create the change I envisioned and, thus, the reason my children (and the world) would inevitably be shorted.

Adopting stories without first examining them is like saying yes to a new pet without knowing what kind of animal you're agreeing to live with. You may end up with a kitten, but it could just as likely be a poison dart frog or a skunk or a mountain gorilla.

By adopting the story that you shouldn't have stretch marks, you may as well be inviting insecurity to join you every time you swim with your kids or try to enjoy sex with your partner.

By adopting the story that you're responsible for your children's happiness, you may as well be inviting guilt and failure to orchestrate your everyday life.

Adopting the story that you should be able to keep up with the pace of the world around you is like asking a mama cheetah (surrounded by her cubs) to keep pace with a runaway train. She may be capable of running that fast, but she and her babies would surely suffer as a result.

My Days As an "Addict"

Looking back on my early days as a mother feels like reflecting on the life of an addict. My intentions were pure (alleviate the suffering of the world), but my thoughts were habitually self-sabotaging. I was addicted to the pursuit of the "right way" to live. I was addicted to proving myself good, strong, determined, and dedicated enough to *deserve* happiness and joy. I was addicted to trying to close all the gaps I possibly could, including those contrived by my unsettled mind and hurting heart. It took "hitting bottom" before I could finally see my mind-set for the endless downward spiral it was.

The idea that I may have been creating my own suffering—based not on my inability to do enough or other people's inability to get their shit together but on unchecked thoughts and the stories born of them—was like a floodlight so bright that even my deeply-buried soul could see it. Maybe I *wasn't* weak or failing or crazy. Maybe I was simply stuck on a set of stories:

- The story that my worth depended upon my accomplishments and level of dedication.
- The story that through self-sacrifice and hard work, I would eventually find my bliss.
- The story that fun is for those who can't see how much work there is to be done in this screwed up world.
- The story that the world is screwed up.
- The story that my girls deserved the best of what life had to offer, and that it was my job to give it to them, whatever the cost to my own well-being.

Rooted in fear and scarcity (which I hid behind dedication and determination), my passions became saboteurs. The shadows of my strengths were running the show, and no amount of *doing* could fill the gap between my accomplishments and the infinite problems I perceived.

Most of the time, we don't even realize we're telling, believing, or otherwise perpetuating less-than-true stories or adopting stories not meant for us. Many are so interwoven within our routines and habits, rooted in family traditions, culturally condoned, and tied up in our sense of security that we rarely think to question them. Our stories are rarely based on facts, but social norms, judgments, suppositions, assumptions, and misunderstandings.

These unexamined stories are *everything* when it comes to the many gaps we feel. And though our culture as we know it depends on us believing otherwise, no amount of shopping, organizing, or Googling is going to make the gaps go way. We don't need any more cellulite creams, snack options, or snap-together storage solutions.

We need to own, examine, untangle ourselves from, and retell our stories.

- Stories about our roles, our value to society, and our importance.
- Stories about what makes us beautiful, successful, and worthy of meeting our needs.
- Stories about what makes us feel fulfilled, alive, and free.
- Stories about our responsibilities, our pain, and what our children need from us most.

We need truer stories told and retold, written and rewritten, crafted, sung, tweeted, blogged, and taken to heart *by* mothers, *about* mothers, in *honor* of mothers, and in the best interests of not only mothers but also all of humanity.

Now, truth is a tricky, triggering word for some people. "True according to whom?" is a valid, important question. Though it means something different to everyone, here's my take on "truth" and the meaning behind the word when used in this book.

Your truth can only be found in *your* heart. You are the only one with access to it. Often, our personal truths are deeply buried beneath other people's perceptions of truth or teachings that claim *the* truth. Discovering our deepest personal truths takes time. It often requires that we sift and sort and drill through crusted-over layers of shame, protection, hurt, and fear. Once we find our truth, however, we have found our internal compass. Our deepest knowing. Our timeless wisdom. Digging that deep is a brave, bold move and one of the most radical acts of love and healing on the planet. You can feel it when you've hit a vein of truth. It feels like absolute resonance. It feels like soul food of the purest sort. It feels like pure light shining on your very essence. It feels like you've finally made your way home.

It also sometimes feels like grief and brings you to your knees with pain and brokenheartedness. This, too, is beautiful. In fact, I've come to see brokenheartedness as one of the best foundations we can possibly build a life upon, assuming that we honor the pain and let it transform us.

How do we do this? We can start by examining our shitty first drafts.

Chapter 5

SHITTY FIRST DRAFTS

The world which men have made isn't working. Something
needs to change. To change the world, we women need first to
change ourselves—and then we need to change the stories we
tell about who we are. The stories we've been living by for the
past few centuries—the stories of male superiority, of progress
and growth and domination—don't serve women and they
certainly don't serve the planet. Stories matter, you see.

—Sharon Blackie

To examine our stories is to bring them into the light. It is to
become conscious of our part in creating them. It is to flag
the thoughts that come up in us *as* thoughts and give them
attention before they become stories that affect our perception of the
world, opinions of others, connections with others, and sense of self.

My favorite process for creating truer stories is one I came across
in the brilliant Brené Brown's book, *Rising Strong*. She was describing

a writing tool originally described by fellow (amazing) author Anne Lamott called the "shitty first draft," or SFD, for short. The shitty first draft is a way for writers to *begin* whatever it is they're working on. These first drafts are messy, unrefined, off-the-top-of-your-head, and quite often, pretty shitty. They aren't the drafts we share, publish, or necessarily feel proud of. They're the ones we work on, refine, and pour our hearts into in order to eventually arrive at the best possible story we know how to tell. Brené explains the usefulness of this tool well beyond the lives of writers. Here's how I use it ...

When I hear, tell others, or tell *myself* a story that doesn't feel good or entirely true for me, I flag it as a shitty first draft:

Babies should sleep through the night. *Shitty first draft.*

My butt is too big. *Shitty first draft.*

People like me less the more self-actualized and self-aware I become. *Shitty first draft.*

My kids are bratty and ungrateful. *Shitty first draft.*

I'm so far behind on this book. *Shitty first draft.*

I write down the SFD, keep it on the table (literally or metaphorically) and create space within myself for a truer version to grow. Over the next hours or days or weeks, I examine the story through a loving, compassionate, and *self*-compassionate lens. Sometimes I ask more questions in order to drill down to deeper truths:

- What is the most generous, loving assumption I can make about the characters in this story, myself included? (Another Brené Brown gem of a tool.)
- What supporting stories have I created in order to back this one?
- How would the oldest, wisest version of myself (my inner crone) tell this story?
- How would someone who knows and loves me deeply tell this story?

- How would it change if I were telling this same story about one of my daughters?

Slowly, and sometimes painfully, I rewrite the story. I know I've reached the truest version I currently have access to when I feel at ease within myself, respectful to all parties, true to my heart, and in-line with my personal integrity.

The thing that strikes me as particularly profound and poignant about this story deconstruction and reconstruction process is that so many people's lives are simply a compilation of shitty first drafts. Shitty first drafts based on long-told cultural stories. Shitty first drafts based on years of self-criticism and knee-jerk reactions. Shitty first drafts passed down from those we love based on their own wounds and dysfunction. Shitty first drafts based on other people's unexamined shitty first drafts!

No wonder so many of us struggle to find joy, ease, connection, and peace of mind.

The Stories We Create Determine How We See the World

Until we moved abroad, my main focus had been on the less-than-true stories *around* me. In fact, for the bulk of my 20s, I recognized so much bullshit in the world that I found little solace in anything *but* my babies.

But the more layers of my stories I pushed through, the more obvious it became that the stories I believed about *myself* had the most impact on my overall quality of life. Beneath every story we tell about the world around us is a story about ourselves in relation to that story of the world. Shifts in *these* stories are where the most profound, affecting change happens. As I've peered, terrified, into the corners of my own soul, and as I've broken open and decided not to close back up, the world looks completely different to me:

- I see mothers scared to death of screwing up and hurting the helpless beings they cherish most.
- I see false promises made by giant corporations, not because they are inherently evil, but because they are rooted in and justified by a false sense of power and the illusion of separation.
- I see a general perception of unworthiness among women of all ages, shapes, sizes, income brackets, races, and levels of culturally-conditioned "success."
- I see self-doubt, confusion, and self-loathing running rampant, based on stories we're surrounded by from birth.
- I see a huge disparity between our actual and our recognized accomplishments and achievements.
- I see potential for change like never before in the whole of human history.

Your stories, however different from my own, are no less powerful in the shaping of your life experience. They affect everything, from the way you see yourself when you stand naked in front of a mirror, to your level of patience when your kids are whining, to your everyday anxieties. They affect your desire for a new house, your craving of another latte, your resentment toward your partner, and your ability to connect with other women.

Consider the stories we've created around feeling overwhelmed. For example, as mothers, we spend a tremendous amount of time and energy attempting to keep our sense of overwhelmedness to a minimum. We plan weeks and months in advance, reduce clutter, cook with crockpots, and buy prepared foods. We choose houses based on closet space, we read books on managing our time, and we pretend we don't need help—when in truth, we've never needed it more.

Why do we attempt to avoid feeling overwhelmed at all costs? Why do we pretend it away when, in truth, we're barely hanging on? I see two reasons:

1. We're told, however indirectly (and from the time we are young), that being overwhelmed is a sign of weakness.
2. Everyone knows that "good moms" aren't weak.

"Good moms" fight overwhelmedness and win. "Good moms" can handle *even more* and still be strong. "Good moms" are creative enough, smart enough, and close enough to a Target to *beat* over-whelmedness and still look Photoshop-fresh.

Consequently (and conveniently), our culture has no shortage of gadgets, methods, creams, pharmaceuticals, appliances, distractions, information, and sales racks to help us keep this feeling at bay (or so they say). Our job as "good mothers" is simply to choose wisely from the hundred million options we're given, make use of our mad skills or the occasional line of credit, and be happy ... because we can ... because we're *free*.

This model of motherhood—one that measures our competency and worthiness by our ability to stay strong in spite of (or in order to overcome) our circumstances—is yet another story we've been told (and sold) in our consume-your-way-to-contentment culture.

Good moms are supposed to avoid feeling overwhelmed. Is this true? Look around you. How many mothers do you know who are successful by this measure? Surely we're not *all* failing as mothers.

Consider the consequences of buying into this particular way of thinking:

- We feel a vague sense of inadequacy or an even stronger sense of failure every time overwhelm sets in.
- We pick up our pace, feel stressed, spend money, and add more to our schedules in order to avoid it.
- We're hard on ourselves, less patient with others, and our happiness is compromised when overwhelm seems impending.

- We consume based on what we're told will help, whether or not the claims are in line with our values or others like them have actually panned out.

By believing the story that overwhelmedness is a feeling to be avoided, we set into motion a way of thinking that affects our experiences, choices, and reactions to the world. The thought breeds further frustration, and avoidance of this feeling becomes our driving motivation.

But what if we were to decide that this story no longer serves us for all the reasons mentioned above? What if we flag it as a shitty first draft? What if instead of interpreting it as we always have, we create a new story based on the way we want to feel?

When I check the story "Good mothers aren't supposed to feel overwhelmed," with not only *reality* but also the truth of my heart, I feel eager to let it go. By bringing awareness to it, I create space for a new story to develop. Here's a story that feels much truer to me:

Motherhood is meant to overwhelm us. It's meant to slow us down and remind us of what matters most. It's meant to expand us in order to make room for the children we're (briefly) given to guide. It's meant to reshape us into fuller, more well-rounded women. It reminds us of our interdependency, shows us where we still need to grow, and strengthens our capacity to connect from the heart.

That fact that motherhood overwhelms us is not a sign of weakness but an indicator of importance. It distinguishes mothering as one of the few endeavors in our lifetime worthy of such an enormous and all-encompassing investment. We are similarly overwhelmed by such things as love, beauty, justice, and the pursuit of a meaningful existence. When we honor the immensity of motherhood as we do other powerful gifts—instead of resisting or trying to tame it—it changes us. Like native trees on a tropical coastline, we have the potential to grow stronger with every storm, thrive when we grow in groups, dance with the wind and waves, and draw our strength from a well deep within.

Now, before you get discouraged, allow me to clarify: I am not dooming us all to an overwhelmingly heavy, frustrating, and draining existence. Though there are aspects of the mothering experience that are meant to overwhelm us, many other aspects are causing undue misery, unnecessary stress, crippling burden, and resentment of the people and circumstances we cherish most. Some of the cultural conditions and conditioning we're faced with as mothers today may be less oppressive than those of our foremothers, but others are actually a great deal *more* oppressive—and certainly more overwhelming.

You Can Change Your Story

We have the freedom to tell a different story about any and every aspect of life that we choose. I'd like nothing more in my lifetime than to see a radical, revolutionary shift in the quality of our stories as mothers. It's about time that *we* be the ones to create our stories, based on our needs, desires, intuition, and inherent wisdom, don't you think?

The story that you're not doing enough isn't even about you. It's a consequence of our society's current obsession with quantity over quality.

The story that stretch marks are unsightly isn't a reflection of truth but a money-making strategy entirely dependent on our feelings of insecurity.

The story that six weeks is plenty of time for postpartum healing, resting, and bonding isn't based on what's best for families but a profits-before-people socioeconomic structure.

Whether you choose to believe popular stories, or own, examine and retell them, determines their impact on your life.

Though it can be difficult to imagine such stories shifting on a cultural level, people said the same thing about slavery, women's suffrage, and the 2,000-year practice of bloodletting. What's more, because women and mothers have always been cultures' natural storytellers, community builders, and new life nurturers, our stories have the potential to set the tone of our culture. They determine the hold big businesses have on our lives, our influence over history in the making, and the well-being of future generations.

In other words, the stories we adopt, believe, and tell as mothers are kind of a big deal.

Until we learn to tell truer ones based on our inherent worthiness, lovability, sufficiency, needs, and true strengths, we're at the mercy of unexamined stories' incredible and indiscriminate impact.

Are we *really* behind in our lives, or have the standards simply been set by those who have no business determining our priorities? Is stress the price we must pay for our freshly-won freedoms as women, or is it simply a consequence of our collective unchecked thoughts? Does information equal obligation, or are we merely out of touch with the incredible capacity for intuitive discernment each of us possesses?

Once we realize where our *actual* power lies—in the expression of who we really are beneath all the stories—we open ourselves to endless joy and potential. Until then, there are plenty of people, corporations, conformists, and inner task masters who are happy to continue telling our stories and determining our quality of life for us.

Byron Katie's question, "Who would you be without your story?" is a powerful one, and one I believe every mother deserves an answer to. But the question I ponder more often at night (during what I've deemed my "How to Heal Humanity Hour," from 2 to 3 a.m.) is this:

What would the *world* look like if you and I—as the first generations of resource-rich, informed, penicillin-protected, and *free* mothers to have ever walked the planet—released ourselves from the burden of stories told for us and began to see ourselves for the incredibly powerful, important, worthy, and inherently beautiful beings we really are?

I believe the outcome would change the course of history.

But because you're probably thinking more along the lines of changing diapers or insurance policies than waging a revolution *today* anyway, let's take this one step at a time.

Let's take a look at some of the main players in *your* life story and examine why it's so easy to get entangled, whether or not your stories are contributing to your health, growth, or fulfillment.

Chapter 6

LOOSENING OUR ENTANGLEMENT

The difficulty lies not so much in developing new ideas as in escaping from old ones.

—John Maynard Keynes

Our society assures us that once we've got our lives all lined up—once the kids are finally all in school and you land the perfect job, once you've shopped and baked and cleaned your way through the holidays, once your countertop grout is de-grimed, grad school is finally behind you, or you finagle a way to finance the new addition—peace will be there, awaiting your arrival like a grandma with a plate of warm cookies.

But is it true? Or is it just a sellable story?

Our deepest longings—for balance, order, connection, love, purpose, presence, and peace of mind—may be satiated for a time through purchases, comforts, and pleasures. But once we've bought the double jogger and our spices are neatly displayed, once we've paid the second mortgage and returned from vacation, when our kid pukes on the new couch, the housing market tanks, or we flip out (again) over their fighting, the search continues. For solace on a sale rack, for balance through our checkbooks and asanas, for order through organized closets and agendas, for just a little more *something* that we know we want, but we can't quite pinpoint.

That something? That thing you long for *way* more than good chocolate or a week in the Caribbean? It's the full, uninhibited expression of your soul. It's the essence of who you are and why you're here. I also believe it to be the thing that your family, and the *world,* needs from you most.

Ironically, though, our families (and "the world") don't exactly encourage our souls' expression. Can you imagine? "Hey, Mom, you really ought to take the weekend away. Go dance and journal and explore your essence for a few days! We'll be fine, and after all, your soul's expression is the greatest gift you could possibly give to us!"

As if.

Even if we did have full permission from our loved ones to explore our souls' longings, many of us would hardly know where to start or where to find our souls in the first place.

There's a legitimate and powerful reason for this: We're so entangled.

Entangled in centuries-old stories rooted in fear and oppression. Entangled in rules and dogma and guilt and blame and shame. Entangled in who we "should be" and "could be" and "might have been, if only ..." Entangled in modern myths designed to keep us longing and striving. Entangled in love and hope and hormones and a whole lot of hurt.

Before I realized the impact of stories on my life, I felt entirely entangled, even trapped, by my circumstances. It was almost as if the same seedlings I had been caring for so intentionally and lovingly had turned out to be invasive species and were now hell-bent on squeezing the soul right out of me. Even their beauty and innocence sometimes felt suffocating.

Now (on my stronger days, at least), I can see that what I'm *really* being sabotaged by in those overwhelming moments are the stories I'm creating *about* my life. I realize that I'm not trapped at all, and that the tendrils that keep growing back over and over again merely indicate stories that I may have trimmed back but not fully discovered and unearthed the roots of.

Though we come by our stories honestly, rarely do we create them *consciously*. Many stories were planted in our subconscious throughout our childhood and have been growing within us ever since. Others are planted within us on a daily basis by marketers in order to turn a profit. The more connected these stories are with our sense of self and self-worth, the more challenging they are to deconstruct.

For the rest of this chapter, we'll take a look at some of the most common origins of the stories we tell ourselves, adopt (whether consciously or not), and allow to shape our lives as individuals and as mothers.

Your Mother's Hand-Me-Downs

From the moment you were born, you've been developing a story about what it means to be a "good" mother. You came into the world biologically wired to expect your own mother to love you, care for you, and meet your most primal needs. Whether or not she did, how she managed, and the way your relationship grew through the years all contributed to this story, to your most primal sense of the maternal and most deeply-rooted sense of yourself.

Like you, your mother excelled in some areas and struggled in others. Her joys, frustrations, and the choices she made were rooted in her awareness of the world and perception of herself within it. You can't fully understand all your mother went through while raising you.

Times were different. Pressures and expectations were different. Women's opportunities, obstacles, and sense of themselves reflected *that* time in history, and depended upon factors such as location, income, education, race, and religious affiliation.

Love it or loathe it, you carry a wide assortment of the stories that your mother held. She grew up forming her own sense of the maternal, of herself, and of the world around her, and then passed these stories down to you, as every mother does. She did the best she could, given what she knew at the time, the circumstances she was living within, her degree of emotional wellness, and the person she believed herself to be.

We form our own stories about who we are and the kinds of mothers we think we should be in large part based on how we felt (and feel) about our own mothers. Such thoughts are quite common and totally normal:

"I should be more involved than she was."

"I should be less strict and more understanding."

"I should play with, cook for, and listen to my kids more than my mom did for me."

Others of us have mostly idyllic memories of our mothers. These (equally limited) recollections often cause us to want to recreate what we had or leave us wondering what we're doing wrong when we can't:

"Mom grew and canned all our food, and I can barely keep a houseplant alive."

"She built a successful career and still managed to cook healthy meals every night."

"Our home was never dirty growing up, and somehow Mom always looked beautiful."

However we remember her and her influence, our perspectives are limited, at best. Between selective memories, the childish understanding from which we developed those memories in the first place, and whether we felt loved and secure or misunderstood and unwanted when the memory was formed, our recollections are more accurately thought of as *perceptions*, rather than facts. This explains why siblings often recall the same event or set of circumstances in completely different ways.

However your mother contributed to your story, you can neither change your history nor the way it has shaped your life until this point. All the resentment, anger, and distance in the world will not erase the facts that make up your history. Likewise, all the longing, nostalgia, and reenactment in the world cannot recreate the joy and sense of wonder unique to your younger years.

Though we can't change the facts, we *can* change the stories we tell ourselves about these facts as well as our responses to them. We'll explore this idea further in the coming chapters.

Other Mothers and Other "Mothers"

As you grew, other mothers contributed to your sense of self, the world, and what it means to be a mother. If you were close to your grandmother, she affected your story line. If you spent lots of time with a nanny, she also shaped your sense of the maternal, whether or not she was a mother herself.

Your early perception of motherhood was also shaped by strangers: the lady in the checkout line who smacked her son for begging, the mom in the cereal commercial who made breakfast feel happy and wholesome, and mothers in fancy suits who worked high-power jobs, raised thriving, witty kids, and still managed to keep their "homes" (aka television studio sets) spotless. Mothers you never even met— from strangers at the store to actresses *posing* as mothers have all shaped your story.

Some of these stories embedded themselves as positive memories, contributing to your overall sense of worth, confidence, and capabilities. Others planted seeds of fear, anxiety, self-loathing, insecurity, and confusion. Both positive and negative imprinting are natural, normal, and happen to us all.

Today, as a mother yourself, your childhood stories have moved from the world of your subconscious to the forefront of your mind. Naturally, because you love your kids and want to be a *good* mother, you ask yourself all the relevant questions:

"Am I doing this right?"

"How do I know if I'm giving them enough?"

"What is she doing that I'm not?"

"Is it supposed to feel this difficult?"

"Am I selfish for wanting to stay home?"

"Am I selfish for wanting to work outside the home?"

"Might they be better off in a more formal 'learning environment'?"

"What's more important: housework or engaging with the kids?"

"Are they safe?"

"How can I possibly know what they truly need?"

Every bit of uncertainty you feel is directly related to your unique story. If your mother worked outside the home and you choose to stay home or vice versa, you may feel the need to justify your decision. If you grew up on TV dinners and Ding Dongs, the idea of serving healthy meals may leave you paralyzed in the vegetable aisle. If your parents were heavy-handed, choosing not to spank may make discipline seem daunting.

As if your childhood influences weren't enough to sort, there's another *huge* reality that affects your perceptions of motherhood and yourself *as* a mother every single day: Everyone wants in on your definition and perception of motherhood.

"Oh, Honey, What a Waste of Your Education"

When my second daughter was a toddler and I decided to work from home in order to keep her with me, a well-intentioned and concerned family member approached me.

"I understand that you'd like to be home with her, but honey, you are college *educated*. I just hate to see you waste your intellect!"

Needless to say, I didn't exactly agree with her sentiment. Though I don't remember my exact response, I do remember how I felt: misunderstood, defensive, angry, and self-righteous. Likely, I either pulled out my soapbox and "enlightened" her as to the naivety in her thinking, or I allowed the comment to sting and drive at least a splinter-sized wedge between us. Today, I am able to see that she was merely telling her own story. She had wanted to go to college but never did. She wanted the best for our family, and to her that meant increased financial stability. She was relating to me based on her perspective, her love, and her desire to justify her own decisions.

We do this to each other all the time.

If your boss can convince you that you're irreplaceable (and your paycheck reflects his sentiments), you may feel quite conflicted about scaling back to part-time hours once your baby is born. If your husband can convince you that you're an awesome cook, he's more likely to be well fed.

Every family member, friend, and stranger you come to know brings their *own* stories to your relationship. Some agree with your decisions, others don't. Some support your parenting style, others are utterly perplexed by it. Often, we don't know, but we make assumptions about the ways people see us.

Depending upon your degree of vulnerability and/or sense of security in the moment, the slightest judgmental glance from a nosy neighbor or raised eyebrow in the baby food aisle will either spark an emotional reaction (which may even send you into a downward spiral of negative thinking) or barely phase you. And because we *often* feel vulnerable, unsupported, and judged as mothers, the former is more common than we likely even realize.

The influence of friends, family, and perfect strangers on our perception of who we are and should be as mothers is powerful and can be quite difficult to untangle ourselves from. Many of these perceptions are grounded in love, security, and partial truths that make unraveling them a complex and complicated process for even the most practiced.

Equally powerful, if not more so, are the stories we all share in common and cannot avoid completely, no matter how hard we try.

Enter ... the big dogs.

The Million-Dollar Definitions

Commercials, billboards, junk mail, magazines, emails, in-store end-of-aisle displays, social media, and sidebars of most every website contribute to your sense of self and experience of motherhood. Marketers don't just want in, they absolutely *depend* on influencing your perception of who you are and "should" be. By convincing you of what you need to be happy, what your family needs to thrive, and personifying a type of mother you might identify with, they are well-positioned to sell you exactly what you "need" in order to fulfill those desires.

The more money you have, the more options are available to you. The more informed you are, the greater your sense of responsibility to make conscientious choices. The resulting indecision can be downright disabling. Conversely, the less money you have, the less options are available to you, and less options means less freedom in your choices. Either way, whether you have tons of money or very little, your experience as a mother is equally influenced by marketing.

Here's where the wool gets even thicker for those of us attempting to live intentionally. Assuming you're aware of the health, social, and environmental benefits of organically grown produce, the next time you're running through the aisles (and assuming the price is right), you're likely to choose the organic carrots over the conventional ones. But what if the price isn't right? What if, because you've decided to stay home with your baby and live on one income, you're on a super-tight budget? The more educated you are, the more aware you may be that not all marketing claims are true to begin with, and that sometimes organic food is shipped from across the world, which might make the local, non-organic choice a better option. You've probably even heard that they bleach baby carrots to keep them from getting slimy. This leaves you once again conflicted, torn between the "right" thing for the environment, the "right" thing for your children's health, and the "right" thing for your family's financial needs. No one way is a sure bet, and you're in a hurry anyway, so you either toss them in the basket and chalk it off as better than the alternative or grab the cheaper, conventional ones and try to ignore the guilt in your gut.

Insubstantial as it may seem, this phenomenon is hardly limited to carrots or grocery store aisles. Most mothers face indecision, guilt, and uncertainty every day, no matter how careful, invested, or intentional we may be. These feelings are the ones relied upon by big business in order to make their billions.

The Prolific Gray

Though by definition, stories are either real or imaginary, many of those being told (and *sold*) within our culture today are not so cut-and-dried. A clever, confusing, and distorted blend of both fact and fiction, more stories than ever are made to *seem* real. Many are so convincing, in fact, that the general populous hardly makes a distinction or discerns the difference.

Walk into any big-box store and you'll be berated by this type of story. While there's no one actually *saying* anything to you, Photoshop "perfected" images, products plastered in promises, nonessentials presented as necessities, items arranged and displayed in ways that "help us" prioritize, and endless suggestions of what is "possible," tell many powerful stories, both boldly and subtly. Back-to-school specials *clearly* equal happier kids, babies *clearly* require loads of gadgets and gear, and according to the sunscreen display, today's beach-worthy moms are calm, collected, petite, free of stretch marks, confident in bikinis, and somehow (even though they're wearing sunscreen), perfectly tan!

This rapidly-growing gray area, which convolutes reality by means of *suggestion*, may not matter so much if the stories were merely intended for entertainment. A woman dressed convincingly as a cat, for example, who really, truly looks feline in nature, is of little threat to us. We don't care that humans can look like cats on occasion. But most stories told these days are not intended for mere entertainment. They are intended to have *influence*.

Influence over our ideas about what's important, valuable, desirable, and possible.

Influence over our sense of self and perceptions of others.

Influence over the way we spend our time and money.

Influence over the way we think and feel.

Though created and distributed by countless sources, the motivation behind this influence is surprisingly simple and universal: to perpetuate a set of beliefs and/or elicit an emotional response. There are deeper motives at play, of course, like power and money and perceived righteousness, but without first appealing to our emotions and beliefs—without a good *story*—all influence is limited.

Our minds aren't evolutionarily accustomed to this degree of trickery, not to mention this *volume* of stories in need of sorting.

In a short period of time (fifty to one hundred years is nothing, evolutionarily speaking) we've had to learn to take in hundreds of times the number of stories on a daily basis, and the gray area is growing:

- Ads are increasingly convincing and customized. Hardly an hour goes by without exposure to marketers' strategically targeted messages of what is beautiful, valuable, and worthy of our time, money, and heart space.

- Social media has us sending and receiving edited stories about who we are and what's possible, further distorting our perception of reality.
- Product loyalty, due to the effectiveness of advertising, has us telling marketers' stories for them. For example, it's no longer simply autumn but "Pumpkin Latte Season."
- Idealized, polished, and seemingly-realistic versions of motherhood are displayed all around us, illuminating the *slightly* less-tidy versions we're actually living.
- Professions we've come to trust with our health and well-being are increasingly influenced by outside agendas. For example, formula samples given to postpartum mothers before they ever leave the hospital tell mothers a story about what's best for their babies, whether or not this story came directly from an expert in infant nutrition.

From these highly influential and prolific stories—stories both interwoven with and often indistinguishable from *true* stories—we form our perceptions of the world and ourselves within it. The story of motherhood, and *mothers themselves* have never been so vulnerable to the influence of twisted truths, partial truths, and flat-out lies in disguise.

We are not only told but also convincingly *sold* the stories of who we are and should be as mothers.

Religion, Traditions, and the Family Way

Every Sunday morning when I was a girl, my mom woke up at the crack of dawn, started the Sunday pot roast, laid out our Sunday best, and prepared herself for "the day of rest." A minister's wife, mother to three daughters, and introverted as a church mouse, my mom didn't have the liberty of a Lord's Day; she was too busy making that possible for everyone else. Between cooking, French braiding, reviewing Sunday school lessons, enduring our whining, finding lost mittens, inverting snow pant legs, and attempting to hide her frustration behind soft curls and a little mascara, then arriving early, pretending to enjoy the perfunctory small talk, performing all the wife-of-a-pastor duties, keeping us quiet during the service, small talking *again* post-sermon, then holding her breath while waiting to hear whether another lost lamb would be joining us for lunch, her week's penance would surely have been paid by Monday morning had we been Catholic.

Whether Jesus himself proclaimed that all little girls must look sweet, their mothers calm and collected, and something savory be stewing during the sermon, he may as well have for the way this family tradition impacted my sense of what it means to be a good mother. The message from my mom was silent but strong: "I'm doing this because it's the right thing to do, but being a good mom on Sundays really sucks."

Now that I'm beyond those early years of motherhood myself, I feel so much compassion and tenderness for my mama when I think back on all she endured. She worked *so hard* to be a "good" mother to us, a "good" homemaker for us, a "good" wife to my dad, and a "good" Christian according to the culture and dogma she was immersed in.

I wish she'd had access to Mary Oliver's poems, "You do not have to be good. You do not have to walk on your knees for a hundred miles through the desert, repenting. You only have to let the soft animal of your body love what it loves,"[6] or Elizabeth Gilbert's Facebook post, in which she questions the wisdom of choosing to be good over choosing to feel free, or even just a close girlfriend with whom she could have been real and messy and imperfect, and still enjoy a deep sense of belonging and acceptance and connection. I wish I could liberate my young mama from the burdens she felt to be "perfect" in order to be seen as "good."

But my mom's journey was (and is) her own, and the influences she's had on my own journey through motherhood and perfectionism have shaped me in ways I'm deeply grateful for. She not only provided me with a rich, wholesome, and nourishing childhood, but her struggle has helped me see the importance of self-love and boundary setting and honoring my intuition, no matter how culturally disregarded or downplayed by the family these things may be. Some of these lessons she taught me directly. Others I learned by watching her struggle, fall, and rise again, stronger.

Your family way, religion, and/or traditions growing up may or may not have looked anything like my own. But scroll back a few years and I'd bet you can come up with a Stressful Sunday equivalent.

Who You Are Apart from Motherhood

The person you are apart from motherhood (yes, that person still exists, whether you've seen her in a while or not) adds yet another layer of variables to your story. The sense of identity you formed before your first baby was born—around your career, relationships, passions, preferences, pastimes, and daydreams—and the ways it has since shifted, all contribute to your story.

If you waited to have children until your career was well established, the new division of your time and energies may be stretching you more than you anticipated.

Perhaps you spent a number of years trying to get pregnant and now feel guilty in the moments your long-awaited gift overwhelms you.

Maybe patience has never been your strong suit, but until their sweet faces were on the receiving end of your hurry, it didn't matter much.

Having started so young, my sense of self was largely formed *as* a mother. Driven by a subconscious need to prove the statistics wrong, I invested heavily in motherhood partly to be sure that, however people perceived me, they would never question my love for and dedication to my girls. Without realizing what was happening (or having any clue as to the long-term consequences), motherhood became my primary source of identity. It never even occurred to me to ask myself who I was *aside* from a mother, or to be sure and honor the whole of who I was, until all the parts of myself I'd been neglecting began to protest—too loudly to ignore.

Whatever your circumstances, your sense of self apart from motherhood (or lack thereof) has no doubt affected your mothering experience in myriad ways.

Attachments, Agreements, Safety, and Acceptance

Some of the strongest, most life-shaping stories in us tend to stem from one of two things: *attachments* to certain people, circumstances, and/or ideas, or *agreements* we've made, whether consciously or not.

For example, if I am strongly attached to the idea that a tidy home is a reflection of my dedication to my family, I am likely to put a ton of effort and energy toward trying to ensure that it stays that way. If I am strongly attached to my father's approval of me as a parent, then I'm likely to make decisions according to what he would think best or shift my ways when he's around.

We form attachments to all kinds of things:

- relationships (whether healthy or not)
- perspectives
- coping strategies
- parenting paradigms
- habits and routines
- thoughts
- ideals

64

- places
- memories (whether accurate or not)
- religious convictions
- aversions
- feelings and emotions
- our sense of identity

The stronger our attachments, the more stories we tend to create, tell, and defend regarding anything and everything associated with the attachment. While some attachments are healthy and essential for our wellness and sense of belonging, many others sabotage us and compromise our relationships in ways we may not even realize. Our inner peace, ability to be the kind of mother we want to be, and sense of wholeness as women require that we examine our attachments and recognize the ways they shape our stories.

Agreements are equally powerful and often harder to recognize. They are perhaps easiest to see in our family dynamics and habitual behaviors. For example, I may feel quite frustrated by the amount of time I spend cleaning up after my children but have a hard time getting them involved in the household chores because I have made an unconscious agreement that I will do the majority of the housework. Another example: I now see that I made an unconscious agreement early on in my experience as a mother to care for my children's needs at the expense of my own. Shifting this story within my family has taken time, caused resistance, and shown me how strongly my sense of self was attached to the perpetual service of others. It took making a different agreement (in this case, an agreement with myself not to ignore my needs any longer) to shift this story for good and in the best interest of the whole family.

It feels important to note that breaking old agreements and putting new ones into place is often a painful, messy process. *It's brave work.* Others within the family unit may not want things to change and may even feel threatened when their own expectations and attachments are questioned. As women pull back the veil and begin to examine, push up against, and reject the status quo, patriarchy and all its many players are pre-programmed to shut us down in order to protect the way it's always been. This is one of the many reasons it's so important to cultivate strong, healthy, empowering connections with other awakening women. We're stronger together and can support one another in times of messy change and tender growth.

Creating attachments and agreements is normal and natural. Doing so helps us meet our most primal, universal needs for a sense of safety and acceptance. But until we examine those we've created unconsciously, chances are, we're entangling *ourselves* and inhibiting our souls' most authentic expression in ways we don't even realize. We're saying "yes" to social and familial structures and stories that dim our light.

Worthiness

Many of our attachments and agreements stem not only from our most primal needs to feel safe and accepted but also our overall self-esteem and sense of worthiness. I may not be particularly fulfilled with my current life circumstances, but until I feel worthy of something better, I'm not likely to put much energy toward changing them. In fact, I may even make agreements that support my story of *unworthiness* in order to make sense of how I feel.

Here's an example that I hear all the time in my coaching practice:

Lucy is completely exhausted and overwhelmed by her three young children and everything that caring for them entails. She is desperate for some time away to refill her cup, but rarely, if ever, gives this time to herself. At first, she explains that she doesn't have the money to hire a babysitter, that her youngest is still nursing, and that she actually loves being home with her kids. She feels that she simply needs to learn to be more patient and stop being so needy. She admits that she used to take time for herself and that she was much happier when she did. Everything shifted once her second baby was born and she decided to quit her job to care for the kids full-time. After we'd explored her story for a while, she became choked up and silent as she stumbled upon an unconscious agreement she'd made: "I am not worthy of meeting my needs unless I'm making money."

Lucy is not alone in this agreement, nor in the association she's made between worthiness and financial contribution to the family.

Examining the story that we must *earn* the right to be loved, accepted, connected, and thriving can have profound effects on our quality of life.

Recently, in MotherWorthy (my yearlong online circle), I posed the question: What do you *almost* feel worthy of?

The answers of the participants were quite telling:

- "I know it sounds crazy, but I *almost* feel worthy of a hot, uninterrupted shower every other day. I dream of showering and blow-drying my hair without anyone demanding a thing from me, but for the life of me, I can't figure out how to make this happen for myself. My husband comes home from work and takes as long as he wants to in the shower while I keep the kids occupied. He's worked so hard all day, so I want to give him this time, but somehow, though I worked hard, too, because I didn't make money, I don't feel worthy of a break."
- "I *almost* feel worthy of charging for my services as a doula. I've been through all the training and mentorship required of me, and know I have a lot to give, yet the idea of charging people for something I love enough to do for free makes me really uncomfortable."
- "I *almost* feel worthy of buying clothes that fit me well and that I feel good in. It just feels selfish to spend money that way when

there are so many other things we need to buy for the house and kids. I'm just tired of feeling so frumpy all the time."

- "I *almost* feel worthy of a weekend away. I don't need to go anywhere extravagant or expensive; I would just love to not be needed for two whole nights. I have no idea why it's so hard for me to ask for such a simple thing. It's almost as if I'm afraid that my family will be fine without me. My entire identity is wrapped up in being needed."

- "I *almost* feel worthy of being able to ask for what I want and need. I know it's not helping anyone to pretend I don't have needs and desires, but asking for more support feels terrifying. What if my husband doesn't see me as worthy of the support I crave? I wish he would just anticipate what I need and hire a babysitter. Then I wouldn't have to question whether or not I'm worthy of it. He would see me as worthy, so I don't have to."

Perhaps the most heart-wrenching worthiness story I hear in my practice is one that I told myself for years. It goes something like this:

"I wanted to stay home with the kids, so who am I to complain now that I'm struggling with it? I signed up for this. I *asked* for this."

The trouble with this story, of course, is that none of us has any idea what we were signing up for when we become a mother. We have no way of knowing what months of sleep deprivation can do to our sanity, what breastfeeding will do to our sex drive, or what letting go of our earning potential will do to our sense of empowerment. We can't know how exhausted we will be by their special needs, dietary restrictions, temperaments, or colic-induced endless crying. We *don't know* what we're signing up for. Hell, we don't even know what we don't know!

Our needs change when we add babies and kids into the mix. *We* change—assuming this change is supported and honored—into wiser, more compassionate, and more self-actualized versions of ourselves. Honoring this shift and recognizing that our needs will continue to change as we grow and face new life circumstances is essential to our wellness as women and mothers. In a healthy, balanced, woman-honoring culture, motherhood would not be a lifelong sentence to poorly met needs, self-denial, and longing for the freedom we once felt but a sacred, supported rite of passage into a rich, fertile, fruitful phase of life.

Motherhood is meant to grow us and affirm our sense of worthiness, not further compromise it.

Unmet Needs

This one is so big that it gets a whole chapter to itself. See chapter 10.

Racial Inequities

Though many of us don't give much thought to the ways in which race and racial inequity affect our perception of motherhood (namely, those of us who are privileged enough that we can afford *not* to think about these things), racial and cultural inequities have a huge impact on many mothers' journeys and stories about motherhood. Disparities between the experiences of white mothers and mothers of color exist within most every daily reality, including income-earning potential, employment opportunities, housing options, health-care access, criminal justice, and access to quality education. Though these realities vary greatly from one mother and community to the next, they must not be underestimated when it comes to the overall narratives we adopt and perpetuate.

The Short of It

Let's break this down. The story of who you are, *think* you are, or think you *should* be as a woman and as a mother is not just some random tale bestowed upon you at birth (yours nor your children's). It is a complex, convoluted *set* of stories, most of which have either been created for you or by you, unconsciously, and influenced by (but not limited to) the following:

- your perception of your own mother
- your perception of other mothers
- your family's religion and longtime traditions
- advertising
- TV shows and movies
- labels assigned to you
- perceived inadequacies
- perceived obligation and duty
- the stories of family and friends
- who you are *apart* from motherhood
- your sense of worthiness
- your attachments and agreements
- unmet needs and repressed desires
- your race

Is it any wonder so many of us feel a little lost?

This bombardment of contradictory stories, opinions, and masterful marketing regarding the most important thing in the world to us—*our families*—makes it next to impossible to answer the aforementioned questions with clarity and certainty.

Am I doing this right? *Who knows!*

How do I know if I'm giving them enough? *I guess I'll just give them more to be safe!*

What is *she* doing right that I'm not? *How would I know? I've never even met her.*

Many mothers (indeed, many humans) stay firmly rooted in unchecked stories their entire lives. For some people, the longer they live, the more adamant they become about defending their stories, because to lose their stories is to lose their sense of self, and thus, their perceived sense of security.

We all know people like this. People whose adherence to dogma supersedes their adherence to the wisdom of their hearts. People who'd rather be told what to do than trust their inner knowing. People terrified of doing things "wrong," for whom misery feels less scary than *vulnerability*.

We know people like this because, on some level, we *are* people like this.

While it's easy to identify unchecked stories in social margins and extremes, we need look no farther than *within ourselves* for thoughts we cling to like life rafts. Safe as they may seem, however, unchecked stories don't perform like life rafts at all. They're more like leaky speedboats with sturdy buckets.

Challenging norms is not the easier path (at least, not initially). Untangling our stories is messy business. But every decision we make comes with consequences, and the consequences of living our lives *without* examining our stories are numerous, profound, and affecting for generations to come.

To get a sense of just *how* affecting, let's take a look at how previous generations have impacted where we are as mothers today.

Chapter 7

OPPRESSION IN A PRETTIER PACKAGE

Freedom cannot be achieved unless women have been emancipated from all forms of oppression.

—Nelson Mandela

Each generation is influenced, both directly and indirectly, by the social norms, schools of thought, hardships, strivings, and fears of the previous generations. The stories told to our mothers about who they were, what made them worthy, beautiful, and successful, and how to be respectable women, mothers, wives, and community members have had a significant impact on our generation.

Just as we are exposed to messages on a daily basis about who we are and who we "should" be, our mothers and grandmothers either absorbed and believed or filtered and resisted the messages of their own eras. From these messages, as well as their daily experiences of love, security, support, struggle, and self-confidence (or lack thereof), each woman created her own stories about herself and the world around her.

No matter how we perceive the mothers in the generation that birthed our own (or the generation before theirs or the generation before theirs), we have no room to judge them. We have no idea what it was to be them.

In her 1963 bestseller *The Feminine Mystique*, Betty Friedan described what so many mothers of her day were feeling. She called it simply, "the problem that has no name," and explained it as such:

> The problem lay buried, unspoken, for many years in the minds of American women. It was a strange stirring, a sense of dissatisfaction, a yearning that women suffered in the middle of the twentieth century in the United States. Each suburban wife struggled with it alone. As she made the beds, shopped for groceries, matched slipcover material, ate peanut butter sandwiches with her children, chauffereured Cub Scouts and Brownies, lay beside her husband at night—she was afraid to ask even of herself the silent question— "Is this all?"[7]

When I read this for the first time, I was dumbfounded. Not by their nameless struggle, but by its similarities to my own. Given all the opportunities, advancements, privileges, and freedoms they've won for us, how was it that I was *still* asking the same question: "Is this stress and insanity management really all there is to the story of motherhood?"

More recently, a friend gave me Anne Morrow Lindbergh's *Gift from the Sea*. A stunning reflection on motherhood in the 1950s, I read it, thinking all the way through, "Wow, this, too, is me." Here's an excerpt:

> With a new awareness, both painful and humorous, I begin to understand why the saints were rarely married women. I am

convinced it has nothing inherently to do, as I once supposed, with chastity or children. It has to do primarily with distractions. The bearing, rearing, feeding, and educating of children; the running of a house with its thousand details; human relationships with their myriad pulls—woman's normal occupations in general run counter to creative life, or contemplative life, or saintly life. The problem is not merely one of *Woman and Career, Woman and the Home, Woman and Independence.* It is more basically: how to remain whole in the midst of the distractions of life; how to remain balanced, no matter what centrifugal forces tend to pull one off center; how to remain strong, no matter what shocks come in at the periphery and tend to crack the hub of the wheel.[8]

Reading each woman's narrative, I couldn't help but wonder why so little has changed, not about the way motherhood *looks*, but about the way it *feels*. We technically have more freedom, but is "free" what we're all feeling?

In order to get a clearer picture of where we're coming from, let's explore the history of motherhood in allegorical terms.

The Mothership of Oppression

Imagine an enormous ship lost at sea. The Mothership, we'll call it (because we can), represents the whole of women's history. The sea represents human consciousness. Aboard this ship are some pretty horrendous circumstances: babies dying of disease; children sold into slavery; abusive, dominant men with free reign over women's bodies and lives; laws preventing women from having a say in meeting their basic needs; restrictively modest clothing; ruthless religious dogma ... you name it.

Also abundant on this ship is love, connection, and joy shared between mothers and children, friends and families, neighbors, and the occasional marriage in which the man is kinder to his wife than socially expected.

The way of life on board is all the women have ever known and, according to their aging relatives, oral traditions, written legends, and folktales, it's the only way life has ever been. There's no expectation of thriving. Women the world over are merely surviving.

Between atrocities, baby-having, child-rearing, and keeping their families alive, the mothers stay plenty busy. They share the daily labor and rely on one another in times of tragedy. They make homes, make connections, and generally "make do." Slowly, over thousands of years, their circumstances improve, if only slightly. Penicillin is discovered and fewer mothers and babies die at birth. Laws are loosened, abusive practices are increasingly frowned upon by the men folk, and women are no longer hung, shunned, or burned alive for speaking out or attempting to improve their circumstances. Their burdens somewhat lifted and their fears of repercussions lessened, women begin to find a little extra time and energy to organize. They speak up, demand change, and want more rights. They take risks, find their voices, and inspire those around them. Despite continued resistance by many, the powers that be eventually grant women some of the freedoms they'd been fighting for. At long last, mothers are no longer limited to the oppressive way of life aboard The Mothership. At long last, they have *options*.

Slowly, a few of the bravest (or most desperate) among them gather what they have and, babies in arms, jump ship into murky but hope-filled waters. They seek jobs outside the home despite the judgment from men and women alike. They ride waves of verbal abuse, emotional manipulation, and isolation. Others stay back, preferring the certainty of *known* oppression to the vastness of the sea of uncertainty. Over the years, more and more women, inspired by the hard-earned successes of those who'd gone before them, follow suit, take a chance, and jump ship.

Thing is, The Mothership is not the only ship afloat on the vast sea of human potential. Right about this time, other enormous ships begin to appear. Flashy ships with color TVs and vacuum cleaners. Ships with indoor kitchens and painkillers and pretty, ready-made clothes. Mothers are thrilled by these new ships, and no one blames them. After all, they've survived their fair share of anguish and deserve a nicety or two.

Pretty soon, there are big, flashy ships everywhere, with modern homes and picket fences and schools and hospitals and grocery stores and more stuff than anyone could possibly ever need.

Before long, nearly every woman who'd jumped (including her now-grown offspring) has found another less-oppressive ship than the one she'd abandoned. Aboard some, mothers work long hours while their children are looked after in daycares. On other ships, women stay home with their children and, too proud or ashamed to complain, bear their burdens alone. Many of those who'd boarded the fancier ships are now burdened by their own possessions, and those who chose speedboats are beginning to realize that their kids are being dragged along behind them.

Perplexed, stressed, and lonely as ever, women on every boat begin to wonder, "Is this it? *This* is what we left The Mothership for?"

Few are happy with their circumstances, but because they're all so different and disconnected, each simply manages the best she can. She buys what she can afford to alleviate her frustrations, gives her children all she's able, and works tirelessly to keep up with increasingly achievement-based measures of success. She takes on more and more to prove herself worthy and "good" by society's increasingly-impossible standards.

Then a crazy thing happens: everyone is suddenly connected via the internet! Women from all kinds of different ships start noticing one another and reaching out. One chat room, blog post, Facebook group, and Instagram story at a time, connections are made by the millions.

"Hey! How's that working out for you?"

"Are we doing this right?"

"Where the hell are we headed anyway?"

The main themes of their conversations? Reconnecting and feeling better, stronger, and less alone in their struggles. By swapping stories, offering empathy, and alleviating one another's loneliness, two things become obvious. First, not everything they left behind on The Mothership was horrible. In fact, some things suddenly seem kind of *essential.* Second, less-oppressed and totally stressed was *not* the goal of the original ship jumpers.

It soon becomes obvious that the real problem lies not in The Mothership itself, but in the masculine, patriarchal, scarcity, and fear-based consciousness they are still afloat on.

So, they round up all the kind, awakening dudes and garden tools they can find, pry the children from their screens, and head to the closest islands of solace, where they cultivate a new consciousness that honors nurturance and compassion and creativity just as much as progress and profit and conquest, and they all live in bliss for the rest of eternity.

The End.

Okay, so the actual ending needs some work and remains to be seen, but the overall points remain:

- We know what we *don't* want of the old models of motherhood.
- We're increasingly clear that the new models aren't delivering either.
- We're finding that some of the things we abandoned (local communities, a sustainable pace, a strong sense of purpose, and respect for home life, etc.) are essential if we want to thrive, not merely survive.
- Just as one set of oppressors was being lifted, capitalism handed us a whole new set, making it much more difficult for us to identify our true needs and desires.
- We have the opportunity to reconnect and reset our sails like never before.

However essential to our collective story, there is no way those women who jumped ship generations ago could have anticipated the consequences of such broad-sweeping and sudden change. They couldn't afford to think like that. They simply gathered all the courage they could muster, held onto their babies best they were able, and took a chance in the interest of future generations.

They took that chance for *our* benefit, ladies. And though our lives are undoubtedly freer, we're still a little lost at sea.

Our Grandmother's Leftovers Are Starting to Stink

Extreme change comes with extreme consequences. One consequence of extreme (and extremely fast) liberation within the world of women is that we're still clearer about what we *don't* want than what we do.

We've known for ages that we didn't want the oppressive circumstances that defined the old paradigms of motherhood:

- We don't want our home lives and families to define us *exclusively*.
- We don't want limitations put on our opportunities and resources.
- We don't want our roles and worth defined by others.
- We don't want to live in perpetual survival mode.
- We don't want to be seen or treated as lesser than or subordinate to men.

But now, having tasted the consequences of the *opposite* extreme—the full swing of the pendulum—we're discovering a whole new set of realities we don't want either:

- We don't want to feel so spread thin that we're emotionally unavailable for our loved ones.

- We don't want to race through our lives and miss the beauty in the everyday.
- We don't want constant stress, obligation, and anxiety as our new norms.
- We don't want to feel disconnected and lonely.
- We don't want to compete with other mothers.
- We don't want to have to "do it all" in order to "prove" ourselves worthy.
- We don't want our "successes" to come at the expense of our families.

So what *do* we want? And why are we so confused as to how to get there?

Because of our entanglement. Because we're still afloat on centuries of unchecked stories and fear-based consciousness.

A look at what was considered culturally acceptable just half a century ago illuminates how far we've come and how fast.

Consider the way women were regarded in the following ads from the 50s and 60s:

- "The harder a woman works, the cuter she looks."
- "Most men ask, 'Is she pretty?' not 'Is she clever?'"
- "Do you still beat your wife? Maybe you should never have stopped."
- "Learn to train your wife in just five easy lessons."
- "She can drink while not voicing her opinion."
- "He said my teeth are so good I can be his receptionist when I grow up."
- "Don't worry darling, you didn't burn the beer."
- "Why spend all that time vacuuming when you still have to cook his dinner?"

- "WIVES. Look this ad over carefully. Circle the items you want for Christmas. Show it to your husband. If he does not go to the store immediately, cry a little. Not a lot. Just a little. He'll go. He'll go."

Our own mothers read these ads as young girls. Their mothers bought the vacuums, toasters, weed killers, cigarettes, and spray starch they were told would improve their difficult lives. *Of course they bought them.* We're all wired the same: to avoid pain and pursue pleasure. What better options did they have?

But the veil is being lifted on this grand illusion, isn't it?

We're beginning to see the emptiness and distraction of their promises.

We're learning that quality of life has less to do with products than it does rich communities and meaningful connections.

We're learning that isolation is too high a price to pay for limitless convenience.

We're learning that success, as it's conventionally measured, fails to take into account what's most important to *us*.

Cultural stories are rarely rewritten as the result of an isolated event. More often, shifts happen as a gradual progression. In the case of women's quality of life, this has meant breaking free of the old (which has been happening for centuries), braving the new and navigating blindly for a while (thanks, mom), feeling the second- and third-generation pains of aimless wandering (here we are!), and then, based on all we've learned along the way, deciding for ourselves what we really want and need to thrive.

You and I, as modern women, are extremely well-positioned to do exactly that. You and I as modern *mothers* have the added, biologically built-in benefits of humility, patience, unconditional love, compassion, and an instinct to protect and nurture. Not only have we never been better positioned to create our collective story however we choose, but the world has never been so hungry for exactly what we have to offer.

There's no doubt about it: mothers are rising.

Before we can create change effectively, confidently, and in ways that contribute to our collective healing, however, we've got to become clear on two things:

1. *Less oppressed* and *extremely stressed* is no place to settle and get comfortable.
2. We're much more capable of changing and bettering the world, if each of us as individuals, are *thriving*, not merely surviving.

Categories of Oppression

I'd be willing to bet that when you hear the word *oppression*, you don't picture your *own* reality but some other poor mama's. Lone pioneer women with abusive husbands were oppressed. Slaves are oppressed. Mothers forced to ration food among their children and still not able to stave off hunger are oppressed.

But not you and I. Because you and I are *free*.

By definition, though, oppression is not limited to "the exercise of authority or power in a burdensome, cruel, or unjust manner." It is also defined as "the feeling of being heavily burdened, mentally or physically, by troubles, adverse conditions, anxiety, etc. ..." Which means that many, if not *most* of us as mothers (and humans) in the developed world get counted, too, if to varying degrees.

In order to better understand our unique place within history (and within the world), I've created three categories of oppression that I believe merit exploring:

- Category 1: Overt Oppression
- Category 2: Covert Oppression
- Category 3: Unconscious Oppression

Category 1: Overt Oppression

Overt Oppression applies to those living within dire conditions that are nearly impossible to change or escape from. The most severe, obvious, and irrefutable of the three, this is the type of oppression we generally associate with the word. Slavery, abject poverty, abusive circumstances, dangerous living conditions, and laws that restrict the rights and freedoms of certain groups of people all fall into this category. People, particularly women with dependent children living within these circumstances, have little to no say in the betterment of their lives and often keep quiet out of fear for their safety and the resulting well-being of their children.

Category 2: Covert Oppression

Covert Oppression is more subtle, hard to pinpoint the source of, and often disguised as something appealing or of benefit. Prevalent in many developed countries (including the US), this type of oppression presents itself as freedom but still falls short in supporting and sustaining the health and well-being of the masses. Examples of this type of oppression include (but are not limited to):

- A "profits before people" economic structure.
- Glamorization of wealth and success by monetary measure.
- An extreme pace of living that encourages stress and anxiety from a young age.
- Sterile and uninspiring working conditions for extremely low wages and benefits given only to those who work full-time.
- A health-care system that favors the wealthy, the white, and the overworked.
- Extreme societal pressure to be "beautiful" according to unrealistic, inhuman standards.

- Millions in marketing backing the misnomer that possessions, wealth, and prestige are the tickets to happiness
- Limits placed on reproductive rights
- Little to no support for the crucial and formative postpartum months and years for mothers, babies, and families
- Widespread social stigmas and misinformation around natural, normal experiences such as birth and breastfeeding
- Grossly underpaid essential positions, such as teaching and social services
- High cost of natural foods and alternative health-care services
- Inaccessibility of mental health treatment
- The absence of villages and the decline of vibrant, connected local communities
- Systemic racism and racial inequities that are frequently minimized and denied by those who benefit from them.

The trouble with Covert Oppression is that we rarely recognize these realities *as* oppressive. This is because women have never had it so good, and compared to much of the world, we feel we have no room to complain. Because advertising has so thoroughly warped our perception of what's desirable, honorable, and possible. Because we're too busy keeping our heads (and our children's heads) above water to even think about such things. Because our perceptions of the world and ourselves within it have been formed within a patriarchy.

There's no question. Those of us in the developed world have it easier than mothers of yesteryear in *many* regards. There's no polio, no wife beating (allowed by law), and no fear of famine, for starters. But because oppression is so deeply ingrained in us, so firmly embedded in our collective consciousness, we scarcely even recognize its continued manifestations.

This leads us to the most hidden oppression of all, which is buried deep within our personal and collective subconscious.

Category 3: Unconscious Oppression

Unconscious oppression, the most pervasive and affecting of all, consists of the narratives we've adopted and agreed to without even realizing it. Born of unchecked thoughts, unconscious agreements, stories rooted in fear, and unhealed personal, familial, and cultural wounds and trauma, all humans are susceptible and at risk. The more we wake up to this type of oppression, the more choice we have in determining the quality of our lives. Old stories can be examined and new stories created. We can move our focus from victimhood to healing. Our soul's truest, most empowered expression becomes possible only when unconscious oppression is brought into the light and tended to with gentleness, compassion, and nonjudgment.

Freeing ourselves from this type of oppression is a lifelong commitment and requires that we catch our oppressive thoughts and examine our shitty first drafts before adopting them as truths.

Oppressive thoughts sound like this:

- "I will never be good enough."
- "Someone else is responsible for my happiness."
- "My body must look differently in order to be sexy or beautiful."
- "Stress and anxiety are normal."
- "My opinions are not important."
- "I need to apologize for having opinions or taking up space."
- "My intuition means nothing compared to the advice of 'experts.'"
- "I'm too broken or messed up to be worthy of love."

Freeing ourselves from these disempowering narratives requires a willingness to examine the ways we contribute to our own suffering. It also often requires that we seek out support for our healing process from counselors, therapists, coaches, support groups, and/or wise elders. The quality of our experience as women and mothers shifts in accordance to our willingness to step out of victimhood and into a more awakened, more self-aware, and more self-compassionate way of thinking and living.

Until we begin to examine every story that strikes a nerve and creates dissonance within us, until we are willing to go through the discomfort and vulnerability of honest self-reflection, messy self-emergence, and courageous connections, we will continue to perpetuate the very oppression we long to be free from.

There will be no "saving" the world until we heal from the heart of the matter. We must start within ourselves and work our way out.

What Maya Mothers Taught Me About Oppression

Before moving to Chiapas (the southernmost and most impoverished state in Mexico), I had a pretty classic, naïve, privileged-white-person take on social justice, if I'm honest. In my mind, the evils of the world were mostly capitalistic in nature, money-hunger was the evil of all evils, and given enough big-hearted aid workers and generous donors to support them, we would surely right all the wrongs sooner than later.

That was before I met Luch.

Luch

Luch was a Maya mother exactly my age. She lived in a one-room cinder block home that resembled a car wash stall, only the ceiling was lower and the adornments more religious. Weeks before I met her, Luch had had a parasite-induced seizure, fallen into her cookfire, and been severely burned from the waist down.

Some friends invited me to accompany them to her home to see how we could help. I was wholly unprepared for what I now see as another turning point in my life.

We showed up in my friend's old van, unloaded a few bags of food, and were greeted by Luch's mother. Dressed from head to toe in hand-spun woven wool and aged twenty years by her missing teeth, she greeted us in broken Spanish, explained our presence to the other family members in her native Tzotzil, and led us to Luch's "bed." Wooden slats cushioned by a single wool blanket cradled her frail and pain-ravished body. She smiled weakly when she saw us, nodded when our presence was explained, and returned once again to enduring the unthinkable.

I don't remember much more about that day aside from the look of longing on her mother's face, the warm and comforting glow of Luch's crackling killer, and the achingly familiar scent of sweat in her mother's embrace when she hugged me goodbye. She did not smell of an unbathed Maya. She smelled like a grief-stricken mother. A mother who'd endured realities I'd never dreamed of. A mother watching her grown daughter die. A mother with no access to a proper shower, much less a way of saving her child due to oppressive circumstances beyond her control.

Doctors don't treat Mayas without money, and Mayas *with* money are as rare as laws to support and protect them.

Luch lived another two weeks on this planet, then planted herself deeply within my heart. The first in-the-flesh human I ever encountered who lived every day of her life under category one oppression, incinerated my poverty relief theories like dry logs on a Maya cookfire.

Crecencia

A year later, I had the opportunity to be a part of a stove project in another impoverished Maya village. The idea was to install vented, efficient wood fire cookstoves in the homes of families most in need, feasibly alleviating a whole host of common problems from respiratory disease to deadly burns such as Luch's. I spent the night with a young family who lived more lavishly than many in their community. Their hillside home consisted of a one-room sleeping shack (separate from their cooking shack), a dilapidated outhouse, and a pig. More than hospitable, Crecencia offered us a place to sleep on the floor of her shack, Nescafé with enough sugar to make it thick, Coca-Cola, and hot tortillas made from fresh-ground masa.

Already blown away by all I was taking in, something unexpectedly powerful happened as we were settling in for the night: Crecencia turned on a tiny black and white television. In poured commercial after commercial promising firmer skin, happier children, and domestic ecstasy for the bargain price of what these people might earn in a month. As the telenovela (soap opera) came on—dramatically depicting the "covetable" lives of the wealthy—I gazed at the faces of my new friends in their beautiful handwoven clothes, breathed the cold night air blowing in between the slats of their wooden walls, and hid my tears behind my tiny plastic cup of probable diabetes.

I wanted to jump up and warn them, "No! You don't want this! We've got it all wrong!" I wanted to stand in front of that stupid TV (threatening the self-sufficiency and contentment of these already-oppressed people) and say, "Look, people in my country are starved for what you have! You raise your kids together and live off the land and practice the arts of your ancestors. Those are riches far more valuable than anything we can buy!"

But then I remembered the young mother who just that morning had shared of her son's death, simply due to the absence of a doctor, and the fact that most of the women I'd met didn't know how to read, and that the "foods" we'd been offered were not only malnourishing but also all they could afford. I sat quietly, forever changed but utterly speechless.

Slowly, I've come to realize why I had nothing to say in that moment: because my purpose there was not to influence their lives but for theirs to influence mine.

Lucia

My love for weaving began in high school. My art teacher was a longtime fiber artist, and over the course of her many years of teaching, she'd built an impressive weaving program and assortment of looms. Awestruck by the art form, I spent as much time learning from her as I could.

My parents gifted me with a floor loom for my high-school graduation present, and my earliest memories as a mother include warping my loom and nursing intermittently, then keeping my daughter's fingers from being pinched while I wove. During my late teens and early 20s, I spent most of my free time weaving, listening to folk music, dreaming of the sheep farm I hoped to one day own (I've since moved on from that dream), and relishing in the sweet interruptions of my curious toddler.

So, you can imagine my excitement when I realized that the Maya community I'd been working in eighteen years later was a community of weavers! Lucia, a mother of three and stove recipient, could be found tied to her backstrap loom on the hillside near her shack every time I visited. When I finally mustered up the courage to ask if she'd be willing to teach me (and offered to pay her), she flashed me a gold-toothed grin, then looked around suspiciously, as if she'd just discovered hidden treasure and knew she'd better protect it.

Over the next few months, and in broken Spanish (Spanish was her second language, too), I learned that she and her children receive monthly rations of beans and corn from government trucks that visit the village once every couple of weeks, that she boils the murky-brown water they collect from a pipe at the bottom of the hill for drinking, that Jesus was the only reason she was still alive, and that she hadn't heard from her husband in nearly eight years, when he left for Florida in hopes of finding work and sending them money.

As she carded the freshly-shorn wool for the blanket she was weaving me, she hummed and fussed at her kids and insisted I eat more tortillas. I gladly obliged and matched her grin with my orthodontia-blessed full set. While my mind was busy being blown, the walls around my heart were shattering to pieces. The disparity was simply too heavy for them to support.

These women fit the bill of that first definition of oppression. The one so hard to escape that few women ever do. But despite their obvious and staggering adversity, I saw more peace and ease in these mothers than I have in any other group of people before or since.

It floored me. I couldn't look away.

I knew they held secrets, and I was determined to learn them. As my Spanish improved, I asked questions the best I could of any villager who would humor me (and amused, most would). I watched closely as mothers cooked and children played and grandmothers beat dirt from rugs. I smiled as they whispered about me and pretended their giggly gossip was the exact wisdom I sought (when, more realistically, they were laughing at my utter naivety). I learned a whole lot from those women and the extreme disparity between their lives and my own.

- I learned that connection is sustenance. That when we have each other, even the greatest of adversity becomes more bearable, lighter, and easier to recover from.
- I learned that women are natural cultivators of community. That there is no shame in this, nor weakness in our interdependence.
- I learned that the "burdens" of making a home, when spread among many, become pleasant pastimes.
- I learned that children thrive when allowed to roam in packs and corralled within the crib of a caring community.
- I learned that when we are intimately connected to them, fire and wood and water and soil and seeds and rain and laughter take on the importance they deserve as life forces and sources of healing.
- I learned that having less sometimes means appreciating more.

- I learned that people need not have much in order to give generously.
- I learned that trash becomes treasure when resources are more limited than time and ingenuity.
- I learned that progress, as defined by technological advancements, control, and power, is an inadequate gauge of human achievement.

More than anything, though, I learned that the severely oppressed of the world are following our lead. They are learning about liberation based on what they see on their salvaged and static-streaked TVs. They can't do much to change their circumstances, and there's not a whole heck of a lot we can do to directly change them either. (That particular stove project created more problems than solutions for those women, by the way). But indirectly? You and I are the ones best positioned to plant the seeds of their eventual freedom.

By living within the "free world" and refusing to settle for *less oppressed* as the ultimate goal, we give them hope, show them what's possible, and model change worth emulating.

By telling the story of motherhood the way *we* want it to be told and based on the essence of who each of us is, we automatically and eventually affect their stories too.

No matter how wholesome and simple, we don't want the lives they live. And whether they know it or not, *they don't want ours either*.

It isn't a middle ground we're seeking; it's a higher ground. It's a model we've not yet seen in recorded history. It's a set of circumstances we've hardly dared to imagine.

In order to get there, oppression must be addressed at its root in the human heart.

A Rite of Passage

Several years ago, author and speaker Sean Stephenson helped me to simplify a crazy-complicated season of my life. His message was profound in its simplicity:

Control is a complete and utter illusion. There are two things and two things only that any of us ever has control over: our interpretations and our reactions.

Not our kids' choices and/or behavior (no matter how many parenting books we read), not their exposure to the world's evils (no matter how hard we try to protect them), and definitely not the aging process (no matter how extensive and expensive our plethora of products).

Our interpretations and our reactions. That's it.

While a terrifying thought on the one hand, it's a huge relief on the other. It means that in any given moment, whenever frustration and overwhelm hit, we have not dozens, but *two* things to consider:

1. How do I choose to interpret this set of circumstances?
2. How will I choose to react?

Mothers today are merely *interpreting* our frustrations based on the stories we've been told (and sold) and reacting the best we know how, based on centuries of patriarchal conditioning.

Herein lies the ticket out of our physical, mental, and emotional trappings. At any given moment, we can choose a more empowering interpretation of our circumstances and a more effective set of reactions than our defaults.

Here's one interpretation of my own:

Today's mothers are overwhelmed not because we're inadequate or broken or too sensitive; we're overwhelmed because we're giving birth to a new era of consciousness, and this baby's coming *fast*. We're overwhelmed not because we're not doing enough, but because we've been brainwashed into believing that we can focus exclusively on the needs and well-being of others and eventually feel fulfilled. We're overwhelmed because we're experiencing not only the struggles inherent to our generation but also the thousands of oppressed generations before ours.

Those women? All the mamas throughout history who were truly powerless to change their life's circumstances? Whose lack of cultural freedom kept their lives entangled, no matter how clear their minds and hearts? They're cheering us on. They're nudging us on to higher ground. Every time you show up courageously and speak your truth, every time you dare to break away from the "shoulds" and honor the stirrings of your soul, those women are right there beside you, whispering wisdom into your heart and breathing strength into your spirit.

We are not alone in this journey, mamas. We are never alone.

A whole new batch of stories is waiting to be born through us: stories that bring us together; stories rooted in our actual importance, worthiness, strengths and needs; and stories that support our continued healing and evolution.

Choosing to be a *conscious* storyteller is a hugely courageous act within a culture that commends unconscious conformity. Brené Brown goes so far as to say that "owning our story and loving ourselves through that process is the bravest thing we'll ever do."[9]

I believe that becoming loving, conscious storytellers is also one of the most *revolutionary* things we can do, not only for ourselves but also for every mother, child, and culture to come.

Here's another interpretation:

Motherwhelm isn't a problem, it's a rite of passage. Once we recognize it as such and honor these intense times (and intense seasons of our lives) for the potential they have to help us get clear on what we want and what no longer serves us, we can use that intensity to our advantage. We can learn to direct our energy toward choices that create the connections, experiences, and ways of life we most deeply desire. We can learn to cultivate healthier, kinder relationships with *ourselves* and, in doing so, model healing and health and empowerment for generations to come.

As you move through the remaining chapters, keep in mind that the truest, most beautiful versions of our stories are not told with certain minds but with wide-open hearts. We are *meant* to be deeply affected and changed by motherhood. We are meant to be softened, humbled, reshaped, repurposed, and made wiser. We're meant to grow, heal, and transform for the good of us all and toward the mother-led consciousness we've been blessed with the honor of birthing.

Chapter 8

REEXAMINING OUR IMPORTANCE

And every day, the world will drag you by the hand, yelling,
"This is important! And this is important! And this is
important! You need to worry about this! And this! And this!"
And each day, it's up to you, to yank your hand back, put it on
your heart and say, "No. This is what's important."

—Iain Thomas

You know your role as a mother is important. Without you,
shit falls apart *fast*. The piles grow taller, the funk more profound, and your loved ones' needs more dire by the minute.

But if you're like most moms, you don't always feel important, particularly during the messier, more draining, and more overwhelming
seasons of your life, when the less-than-glamorous aspects of motherhood take up the bulk of your time and energy.

When meeting someone for the first time, you may even find yourself spinning your story in such a way that motherhood seems lower on your priority list than it actually is.

Our answers to the common question, "So, what do you do?" reveal a great deal about how we see ourselves ...

"Oh, I'm a teacher, but I'm staying home with my baby for a while."

"Right now I'm doing the mom thing, but normally, I work as an attorney."

"I'm a writer, so I work from home. Oh, and I have four kids."

Rarely does a mother beam with pride while admitting to motherhood. She may glow when speaking of her children, but motherhood *itself* is often passed over like a shameful secret.

Why is this? Why is it that though we know our roles are important—even vital—we feel the need to make it clear that we are more than "just" mothers?

Here's my two-part theory:

1. We're experiencing a collective identity crisis.
2. The priorities of our culture are drastically obscuring our sense of importance.

Allow me to elaborate.

Our Collective Identity Crisis

Think back for a moment to a point in history that's always fascinated you (say, pre-1900s). Now imagine yourself living as a mother within that time period. Maybe you've been part of a wagon train for six grueling months. Perhaps you've been working extra-long hours in order to keep your kids in school and out of the fields or mines. Maybe you had it better than most and could afford not only shoes for your children but also a handful of books. Whatever the circumstances (assuming you were among the working class), your everyday life would have consisted of more or less the same elements:

- Hunting, gathering, planting, harvesting, storing, or trading food *to keep your family from starving.*
- Making, mending, repurposing, and restoring *to keep your children from freezing.*
- Washing, beating, soaking, wringing, scouring, and boiling *to keep disease, bedbugs, and lice to a minimum.*
- Enforcing rules, punishing misbehavior, and making sure their chores got done right, *because the children's help and submission were essential to the family's survival.*
- Praying to God to spare your lives *because hope in something greater and better kept you from going crazy.*

Fast forward to your life today. Same kids, same position as a mother, only the elements of your everyday life look and feel a little different. Likely, you spend your days:

- Shopping because you're low on groceries, bored of your current wardrobe, or feeling unfulfilled, in general.
- Running kids all over town for practices, lessons, and playdates.
- Playing with your kids to keep the guilt at bay.
- Googling solutions to all your problems to minimize your anxiety.
- Trying to be patient with your kids' entitled attitudes because "putting them in their place" is no longer an acceptable way to parent.
- Making things because you need a hobby and want a handmade feel in your home.
- Catching up on the laundry or dishes because no one has any clean underwear or spoons for their cereal.

Dramatic oversimplification or not, the point is that mothers of yesteryear, however difficult their daily lives, had one distinct advantage over us: their positions came with an inherent sense of importance. *They ensured the survival of the species.*

We, on the other hand, spend the bulk of our time trying to ensure our *sanity*.

I saw this distinction, too, among the Maya mothers in Mexico. They don't doubt whether it's worth their time to collect firewood so their kids can eat. There's no inner debate over whether or not they should (hand) wash the only change of clothes they own aside from the ones they're wearing. Harvesting the corn that will feed their families for the better part of the year is not merely worthwhile but also vital to their children's survival.

But because the majority of us are fortunate enough not to have to think in terms of life or death decisions every day, we're faced with the daunting task (whether we realize it or not) of cultivating a sense of purpose and defending the relevance of our positions.

What are we *really* worth to our families (and society) now that nearly every job we used to perform can be done better by an appliance, specialist, gadget, or minimum-wage employee?

If not survival of the species, what gives our positions relevance and our daily lives true and lasting meaning?

Making milk while other women make millions hardly seems like something to brag about.

Organizing the bake sale while other women fight for social justice almost seems silly.

Reading *Little Bear* (for the hundredth time) when we know other women are reading medical charts can leave us questioning our prioritization, even our worth.

Survival mode comes with an inherent sense of purpose and determines our priorities for us. Clearly this does not mean that severely oppressed mothers had (or have) it better than we do. What it does mean is that we are frontierswomen when it comes to navigating these complex and confusing times. It's the Wild West in regards to our relevance.

This is hardly helped by the fact that as our society defines importance, motherhood lies outside the margins.

Importance According to "Them"

Making choices has never been more challenging. Decision fatigue is very real and very much a part of many mothers' everyday reality. How are we to know what, of all the million products, experiences, and pursuits, is worthy of our time and energy?

We decide what's most important based on the unique and varied stories we've cultivated and accumulated over a lifetime. The confusion comes in when we look around us and realize how many other versions are possible. We notice someone's passion or sense of purpose, a company's promise or commitment to a value that resonates with us, and wonder whether we ought to reconsider our position or add to our plates. Might our time be better spent some other way?

- Is it more important to keep the house clean or the kids engaged?
- Is it more important to save for retirement or live your dreams while you're young?
- Is it more important to give them a holistic education or exposure to racial diversity?
- Is it more important to offer financial stability or the stability of a stay-at-home parent?
- Is it more important to save the environment or your daily sanity?
- Is it more important to choose organic or locally grown?
- Is it more important that your needs or *theirs* be met in this moment?

Ask ten different people the above questions and you'll not only get ten different sets of answers but likely a handful of strongly-defended opinions.

We've been taught our whole lives to associate importance with things like:

- making money
- the acquisition of nice things
- power and prestige
- efficiency and speed
- measurable progress
- whatever's currently "cool"

Though all these goals are presented as *possible* within the world of motherhood, most every mother I know who measures her worth according to these standards feels behind, insane, or defeated.

In fact, by most of these measures, motherhood is practically the antithesis of what's most important:

- It's unpaid.
- It's vulnerable.
- It's messy.
- It's immeasurable.
- Its rewards are largely intangible.
- It's not exactly cool.

Even within more countercultural circles, importance is measured in ways that don't always seem to mesh with motherhood:

- sustainability
- social justice
- minimalism
- adventure

- balance
- self-sufficiency
- spiritual enlightenment

Have you ever tried raising a mess of kids while striving for efficiency, consuming minimally, saving money, adventuring, making everything yourself, and fighting for social justice while staying balanced and spiritually centered?

I have. It feels anything *but* sustainable.

By allowing the world to define our importance for us, we subject ourselves to constant bombardment of obligations, guilt, stress, deep disappointment (in ourselves, above all else), and a disabling sense of inadequacy.

Claiming the right to decide what is most important, and what makes *us* important as mothers and unique individuals, is essential to shifting the many burdensome stories affecting us all.

We must reclaim motherhood from those who've reduced its relevancy and cheapened cultural definitions of its worth. Marianne Williamson's proclamation about womanhood must also be applied to motherhood, "We can't look to the world to restore our worth; we're here to restore our worth to the world."[10]

Despite our wrestling with relevance, deep down, we *know* that our roles are essential. This is because we don't merely learn but *intuit* our importance.

Our intuition tells us that nurturing matters just as much, if not more than making money.

Our intuition tells us that our children's wellness is an invaluable investment.

Our intuition tells us that we are powerful beyond measure *by way of* the maternal.

Our intuition tells us that we are the cornerstone to the sustainability and health of any society.

Our intuition tells us that the foundation of equality, justice, and peace is a secure, supported, and love-filled childhood.

Yet because the loudest voices in our culture are not coming from us but from moneymakers and power seekers, we rarely receive validation in line with this inner knowing. We then seek to increase our *sense* of importance by allowing those who *seem* to have our desires and best interests in mind to lead us.

- We consume well beyond our needs and attempt to keep up with the latest trends.
- We pick up the pace and beat ourselves up when we "fall behind."
- We put our faith in "experts," ignoring our gut instincts.
- We focus on outcomes, hiding and ashamed of the messiness of our journeys.
- We deny or minimize our needs for support and connection in an effort to come across as independent and self-sufficient.

Then, when we still don't feel fulfilled, we wonder where we've gone wrong and add more in an effort to compensate. Stuck in yet another story loop, we spend as much time trying to feel good as we do questioning our legitimacy.

Is motherhood just inherently *menial*? Must we find our meaning in the mundane and worth in the sum of our sacrifices? We certainly can, and we'd not be the first generation to do so, but we can also choose a different *interpretation* of our importance and a different set of *reactions* than the ones contributing to our confusion.

Our Actual Importance

A huge percentage of our lives as humans is spent doing seemingly insignificant, seemingly unimportant things. Even the most intentional and enlightened among us still have to clean out our cars and shop for printer cartridges, after all.

Mothers have even more of these tasks on our plates than everyone else. We're responsible not only for our own daily "drudgeries" but also the never-ending needs of everyone who depends on us. Between diapers and dishes, screen time monitoring and meltdowns, how can we possibly find time (or energy) for what's most important by *any* standard, much less those required to save the world and heal humanity?

This is the heart of where our collective story stands to shift.

In every single moment as mothers, we are modeling human behavior, shaping awareness, and affecting change. Whether we're cleaning dog poop from tennis shoes or doctoring a bloodied chin, impressionable, interested, and intelligent young humans are paying attention. Stories are forming. Hearts are being held. Consciousness is being born.

There's nothing menial about it.

When my teenager runs in the room, freaking out about what she should wear to dinner with her boyfriend's family, I am not merely being called upon to play fashion police (if you knew me, you'd laugh at the very idea). I'm also being entrusted with someone's fragile and emerging sense of self. If I choose to see beneath the obvious cultural measure of importance to my own *maternal measure*, I might sense several things: a need to be affirmed for her lovability, a desire to be seen for her inherent beauty, and a self-consciousness around her changing body. In that moment, there is nothing menial about what I'm doing. I'm validating someone's self-worth.

When my 13-year-old screams in horror as her sister barges into the bathroom, I'm not merely being called upon to remove the perpetrator and set things straight but also to affirm her sense of justice, respect, and healthy boundaries. I'm honoring her intuition so that she'll know how.

When my 15-year-old responds sassily to something I say, I'm not merely needed to correct rude behavior but also to teach effective, compassionate communication. She's asking me where the limits are. She's trying to figure out what to do with strong feelings she's not yet learned to manage. I'm creating a safe space for her to discover herself, practice using her voice, and refine her strengths.

When I receive a text from my grown daughter that includes photos of her new vacuum cleaner and handmade Christmas decorations, I see right past domesticity and holiday spirit. I see self-emergence, kindred creativity, and a desire to be seen as an equal. By validating her as beautifully, wholly independent of me, I am not merely making peace with letting her go but also equipping her with the confidence she needs to create a life she loves.

It's no different in your own "menial" moments.

When you respond to your baby's cries in the middle of the night, you are not merely enduring sleep deprivation, you are also shaping her most primal sense of security—the same sense of security that will sustain her throughout her entire life.

When you listen to his long-winded tales about superheroes and Minecraft, you're not merely validating his interests but you are also teaching him what it feels like to be heard by someone who loves him deeply.

When you give birthday gifts only a grandma can get away with, you are not simply doing your duty but also widening their circle of love, expanding their sense of safety, and speaking directly into the hearts of the emerging generation.

We are a *big deal,* mamas. I would even go so far as to say that modern-day mothers—the consumers, voters, value-shapers, lovers, and story weavers we are—are among the most influential forces on the planet.

- We are healers of humanity's wounds and dysfunction.
- We are nurturers of strengths and courage and confidence.

- We are cultivators of emotional intelligence and self-awareness.
- We are guardians of The Sacred Feminine and better equipped than any one group of women throughout history to promote and perpetuate Her direly-needed emergence.

This makes motherhood one of the most important roles in the healing of humanity. It's a position of incredible honor, strength, and power ... assuming we know how powerful we really are.

That Which Matters Most

I wonder what Goethe had in mind a couple hundred years ago when he said, "Things which matter most must never be at the mercy of things which matter least."[11] Whatever it was, I doubt he had any idea how relevant his sentiment would still be centuries later:

- How difficult it would become to tell the difference.
- How distracted we would be by the sheer volume of The Unimportant.
- How loud and bold and in-your-face the lies of the least could be yelled.
- How much *profit* would come to shape our sensibilities.

Shifting our stories regarding our importance and the importance of all we do starts with recognizing that *that which matters least* occupies a much greater percentage of our experiences than we realize. Clearly, there is no accurate measure for such a thing, but if I had to guess, I'd estimate that 98 percent of all we're forced to filter falls into this category, making *that which matters most* super difficult to see, hear, and *feel* because of the madness surrounding it. And because that 98 percent is where the profits are made, the other 2 percent is not only hard to hear but also dependent on those of us who *can* hear it to preserve and protect it.

I'd argue, all day long, that mothers—more than any other demographic on the planet—are *wired* to hear that soft-spoken 2 percent.

We hear it when they run for the road and we make like a lioness after them.

Our breasts physically respond to it, making perfect food in perfect time with their cues.

Our hearts are attuned to it, evident by our willingness to sacrifice our well-being for theirs.

Loving, protecting, supporting, healing, and helping to thrive are things we must revere as invaluable, sacred, essential acts. They are fundamental, humanity-shaping gifts that only we can give. No one else is wired for the job quite like we are. No one else is more biologically capable.

Mothers are not mere madness managers and schedule minders. We are the chosen keepers of a quiet, timeless order. A natural, essential rhythm. A sacred evolution of heart-connection and consciousness and healing.

Ours is a uniquely-beautiful challenge in this maddeningly measured culture. We must first hear our intuition (above the noise all around and within us), then come to trust it. Over time, as we begin to recognize the wisdom of our hearts' quiet knowing, our confidence builds and the 98 percent becomes easier to see for the smoke screen it really is.

We do this in ways completely counter to what we've been taught:

- By honoring the sacredness in small things.
- By setting our own pace and believing it's plenty fast enough.
- By recognizing profundity in the mundane and progress in everyday rhythm.
- By defining success and progress and wealth and value for ourselves.

- By realizing how much our children need us, not as chauffeurs and cleaning ladies but as peacemakers, heart-holders, and story catchers.
- By caring fiercely for ourselves, first and foremost, so that we'll have what it takes to care fiercely for others.
- By cultivating self-awareness and learning our unique blueprint for thriving.
- By connecting courageously, openly, and often with other women on the path of personal and spiritual growth.

By silencing the nonessential noise and listening instead to the all-important 2 percent within us, we align our sense of importance with our truest, highest self.

When our sense of importance springs from a well of true personal power and authenticity, we no longer doubt our importance because we deeply *feel* it. And when our work feels important, we're more likely to be invested in, energized by, and enthusiastic about what we're doing. We begin to invest from a place of passion and joy as opposed to obligation and guilt.

The more practiced we become at honoring our souls' sense of what matters most, the more clear it becomes that society's priorities don't often tap into the *essence* of life.

Part of what makes us so important is that we feel and see that essence. We're biologically wired to protect it.

Our Ever-Shifting Sense of Importance

I find my sense of importance as a mother *these days* by reading between the lines, listening deeply for unspoken needs, empathizing, and helping my girls get clear when they're confused. Sure, I also make meals and clean toilets and read books and break up fights, but these in no way define the essence of who I am to my daughters. They will not remember me for the fact that I wake up every morning and creatively pack lunches from whatever I can find in the fridge. More likely, they will remember me for the openhearted, nonjudgmental space I hold for them and their struggles, for recognizing and honoring their strengths, and for refusing to allow the world to define them and reduce their sense of self-worth. I am also committed to modeling wholeness and thriving for them in my own life.

When they were babies, I felt important in different ways. Our bodies worked in sync. My breasts swelled in time with their hungry whimpers. I gained immeasurable satisfaction through creating a homelife that felt wholesome and creative and peaceful. I felt essential because for a short, sweet time, I was the single most valuable person in their world.

This is not a static concept. Our sense of what matters most depends on many factors, including the stage of our children's development, our current life circumstances, the season of our lives, our hormone levels, and the uniqueness of each day.

Some days the most essential thing is that we get a shower and brush our teeth before getting back into bed with our newborn.

Some seasons, the most essential thing is that we become gainfully employed in order to get on our feet, financially, and step ourselves out of an emotionally abusive relationship.

Some years, the most important thing is to act courageously and do that thing we're so terrified of.

Sometimes, the most essential thing is to stop acting so damn put together and start asking for help.

Some days, the most important thing we can do is keep our hearts open and allow the pain to pass through.

As our roles are shifting (faster than evolution can possibly keep up) from surviving diseases and plagues to protecting ourselves from the bombardment of information and overstimulation, mothers are the ones on the front lines and in the trenches. We are the ones experiencing firsthand the effects of our capitalist, patriarchal, soul-starved culture, and doing all we can to protect our babies from it.

Our collective wellness depends on mothers' intuitive sense of importance. Honoring that knowledge and acting accordingly is an act of social rebellion and responsibility.

Motherhood has been represented as something it's not and will never be. It isn't tidy and organized and effortless, nor is it always happy and blissful and serene. Motherhood is real and raw and quite often, ridiculous. It's exhausting and perplexing and different with every child and passing day. It's overwhelmingly difficult and overwhelmingly beautiful all at once. It's packed full of paradox.

Once we get clear, however, about its immeasurable importance, the everyday elements of our existence take on a whole new meaning, and more space can be created for the continued emergence of The Sacred Feminine. Getting clear requires letting go of what other people think we *should* do. Obeying The Shoulds leads us away from, rather than toward, our most powerful, authentic expression.

Chapter 9

FREEING OURSELVES FROM "THE SHOULDS"

When we create a life based on what we think we are supposed
to do rather than from our own heart's desire, we always feel
like something is missing, that we are not quite free. There
is a deeper longing that keeps calling us to stop conforming,
to break the chains of our fears, to jump the fence of people's
opinions and find our innate wild happiness.

—HEATHERASH AMARA

I sighed inside and cringed a little as my new client described her
first encounter with me a dozen years ago: "The first time I saw
you was in the auditorium. You were listening to the lecture while
taking notes, knitting, *and* nursing your baby. 'Wow,' I thought, 'now
she is an Earth Mama.'"

Though it wasn't uncommon to see a mother creatively multitasking at the alternative school our children attended, I was among

the handful rarely *not* juggling babies and projects and information absorption all at once (in the name of all things holistic).

While I cherish my memories of those baby-raising days, they also bring feelings of sadness, relief, and compassion for that younger, "ultra-earthy" version of myself. What my sweet new client couldn't see was that beneath all that well-intentioned multitasking and dedication, I was drowning in my ideals, holding myself to tyrannical standards, and committed to the well-being of others, no matter the cost to my own.

I wasn't knitting and note-taking and nursing all at once because I was a badass with Waldorfian superpowers, but because I was tortured by my inability to make a greater difference, and staying busy helped numb the pain of my perceived inadequacies.

While my natural, homespun ways *were* a reflection of my values, they also provided a really good hiding place. The obvious importance of all I was doing to improve the state of the world and better the lives of my children made it even easier to justify the denial of my own needs.

"Earth Mamas" *should* be doing more than everyone else, I reasoned. My degree of investment surely proved my degree of dedication; and my dedication proved my worth. Any focus on myself was weakness, selfishness, and time that could be spent *making a difference*.

Several times a day, a meek, soft voice inside me would plead for a little attention. Almost immediately, another, more powerful voice would put her back in her place, "Really, Beth? You really think your need for alone time matters more than your baby's need for security through constant connection?" or "You're already slacking on the home-cooked meals and gardening. The least you can do for your beautiful daughters is knit them hats and matching mittens for Christmas."

So, I would pick up my exhausted, spit up-smeared self off the couch, sling the baby, and get back to work.

On the days when I was desperate and drained enough to actually *consider* doing something for myself, all I had to do was touch on a nerve of pain buried within me and I'd recoil in shame. No matter how depleted I felt, Earth Mama beat Scared Shitless of Screwing Things Up Mama, Disconnected from Her Deepest Desires Mama, Miserable In Her Marriage Mama, or Mama Whose Soul Was Starving.

I guess I figured it was better to master the art of self-denial than to turn our lives into a shit-storm of maternal madness, and it was *clearly* more loving to carry the burden myself than to spread it among those I loved and would die to protect.

As long as there were a million needs to be met around me, I was safe. As long as I obeyed The Shoulds, I could keep from being eaten alive by the watchdogs within that snarled at me every time I sat down.

Obeying "The Shoulds"

Whatever's on your list of "shoulds," your own inner task master is no doubt relentless, obnoxious, and/or mean-spirited about *something*. Perhaps she tells you that ...

- You should be more organized.
- You should be more fit.
- You should be less talkative and more punctual.
- You should make it yourself, bake it yourself, or can it with customized labels.
- You should coach their sports teams.
- You should save more for retirement.
- You should be documenting their every achievement.
- You should make more money, more friends, and the daily bread from scratch.
- You should be cleaning instead of napping.
- You should have known better.
- You should have been able to protect them.
- You should have seen this coming.
- You should enjoy mothering more.

Whether they slyly stalk your self-esteem from the corners of your subconscious or wake you up in a state of near panic every morning, thoughts of who you should be and what you should be doing differently have a near-constant effect on many mothers' lives. Our actions, reactions, perceptions of ourselves and others, sense of success or failure, and happiness and inner peace all seem to hinge on our ability or inability to meet these expectations. The stronger our convictions or adherence to a "right" way of living, the more "shoulds" we likely have on our list.

The identities we take on and project as mothers play a powerful part in the creation of these lengthy and burdensome lists. We categorize ourselves and one another (often unconsciously) based on our parenting styles, choices, preferences, and demographics. Once categorized, we determine what we "should" be doing in order to prove or disprove the assigned label. Chances are that you identify with or have been labeled as at least one of the following:

- Single Mom
- Soccer Mom
- Helicopter Mom
- Teenage Mom
- Crunchy Mom
- Mom of Multiples
- Supermom
- Working Mom
- Overprotective Mom
- Stay-at-Home Mom
- Cry-It-Out Mom
- Attached Mom
- Crafty Mom
- One of "Those" Moms

Or in my case, Earth Mama.

Not only is there a label for "your kind," but you'll also find both adamant supporters *and haters* with equally passionate arguments for and against your choices. Because of our conditioning and insecurities (among other things), people find comfort in compartmentalizing one another and implying (or telling you directly) how you "should" be living your life:

You should be paying closer attention to your child on the playground.
She should know better than to let him have an iPhone.
You should wear your baby, nurse your baby, or let him cry himself to sleep.
You should limit their intake of sugar of all kinds.
You should homeschool.
You should vaccinate, go back to work, or give him up for adoption.

Whether or not we buy into the labels, judgments, and opinions of others, we're usually affected by them. Even when we feel solid about our decisions, the suggestion that there's a better way that we aren't choosing rouses one of our deepest fears: that we are somehow harming or shorting the humans we love most.

In an effort to feel better when we fall short or make sure that we don't, we then add even more "shoulds" to our lists. Before we know it, we've developed the habit of dropping "should bombs" all over our lives:

My house should stay clean.
Their toys should be natural.
Our food should be organic.
We should have invested sooner.

I should be able to get more done in a day's time.
The neighbors should mow their yard.
My family should be more conscientious.
They should be more sensitive.
We should go home for Christmas.

And of course, because we love them and want the best for them, we also "should" all over our kids:

He should be kinder.
She should be reading sooner.
She should eat what I cook and be grateful.
He should be sleeping through the night.
She should do chores without complaining.

Add to that all the things we assume should be different within our culture:

Public schools should have healthier lunches and more play time.
Breastfeeding should be more widely accepted and supported.
Part-time work should be more abundant and include benefits.
Health care should be more affordable and easier to apply for.
People should be less interested in their phones than the people
around them.

It's a wonder we're not all protesting procreation!

This mind-set that life should be different than it is or that we should be doing more is one of the strongest, most impactful set of stories being told. Though many such perceptions *feel* like truths, the greater the disparity between our perception of the way life should be and the way it really is—that is, the greater the gap—the greater our overall sense of frustration, failure, and disappointment will be.

Whether we're disappointed with ourselves, those around us, or the world at large, our inner peace is compromised.

Though a phenomenon affecting every demographic within our culture, I daresay mothers feel the weight of this story more than most. Not only should we be on top of and anticipating every last detail in our complex and busy lives, but clearly we should also offer the very best to our children! The more unsettled we feel about the state of the world, the more we feel we must compensate in an effort to protect them.

During my well-intentioned Earth Mama days, my "shoulding" was off the charts. Not only did I carry the weight of all the things I felt I ought to be doing as a "good mother," but I also believed that because I was an intentional and creative environmentalist/humanitarian who'd been blessed with a loving, nature-filled childhood, passions, talents, and a college education, I should also be:

- Volunteering as a breastfeeding consultant
- Making all the Christmas presents/wrapping paper/decorations myself
- Driving my kids to soccer/gymnastics/guitar/drama/art lessons
- Singing in the parent/child community choir
- Teaching my girls to sew/knit/paint/felt/garden/cook
- Keeping a garden/chickens
- Creating a fabric line to accompany my organic children's clothing line
- Teaching classes to bring in money
- Improving the efficiency of our home
- Regularly exposing my kids to wilderness
- Planning for grad school
- Eating and preparing the healthiest, most body- and earth-conscious foods possible

- Baking for new mamas and sick neighbors
- Putting up food for the winter
- Planning elaborate (and earth-friendly and original) birthday parties
- Donating to worthy causes
- Creating community
- Celebrating the seasons
- Purchasing consciously, minimally, thoughtfully, *and* in a way that respected our crazy-tight budget

As soon as I would accomplish one thing I should be doing, another would take its place. The more I learned of a child's needs, my body's dietary preferences, a new local farmers market, a friend with cracked nipples, or a more conscientious way to do something, the more I piled on my plate.

It was absolute crazy-making, but compromise seemed the only alternative, and compromise was *clearly* a cop-out.

I remember wishing that I could just pause my life for a month, catch up with everything I felt behind on, then press play again, with everything organized, creatively adorned, paid, stacked, filed, and freshly painted.

Though Byron Katie taught me to check my stories, it took moving to Mexico to realize how much my "shoulding" was impacting not only my experience of motherhood and overall quality of life but also my effectiveness in creating the change driving my ideals to begin with. Freed from the majority of our possessions (and thus piles and projects that constantly reminded me of all I'd yet to accomplish), I started to see how many of these "shoulds" were not actually essential or enriching my life. Away from friends and family, living at quarter speed (and without a car!), and in a language I didn't speak, my life hardly felt like my own. Suddenly, everything I once thought I should be doing seemed a little ... ridiculous.

Should my girls learn to sew just because my mother taught me? Or might it be okay if we simply walked the cobblestone streets and marveled over the Mayan markets?

Should I cook everything from scratch? Or might the local taco vendors benefit from our patronage and pesos?

Should I make and send Christmas presents for the entire extended family? Or might it be okay to opt out of gift exchanges and be more present with my husband and daughters?

Should I accomplish several miracles before noon? Or might it be okay simply to notice the miracles already being accomplished around me?

Surrounded by poverty-stricken Maya mamas whose lists of "shoulds" seemed even fewer than their freedoms, I began to see my own "shoulds" for what they really were:

1. Products of a culture driven by consumerism and advertising.
2. Notions of value and importance based on limiting, fear-based thinking.
3. Thieves of present-moment joy.
4. Obstacles in the way of my authenticity.
5. Attempts to *earn* the love and joy and sense of worthiness I craved.
6. Unchecked assumptions of responsibility.
7. Shitty first drafts.
8. Evidence of privilege.
9. Unconscious agreements that lead to self-oppression.

With every year abroad came a deeper understanding of how burdened I had been by my own mental constructs. The new-to-me notion that I didn't have to organize or control every last detail of my life in order for it (or for *me*) to be good, was revolutionary. I began to realize the utter limitlessness to what it means to be a "good" mother and how limited I felt within the Earth Mama identity I had constructed in order to feel adequate and worthy. Though I had no idea where I was headed or who I was becoming, I was being reunited with long-lost parts of myself that I was not about to lose sight of again. With my wholeness on the horizon, I followed my hurting heart into the mystery.

Why Should-ing Doesn't Serve Us

Let's take a look at a few reasons this "should" mentality doesn't serve us as mothers:

- *It sets us up to fail from the start.* When is the last time your "should" list actually delivered the sense of completion and peace of mind you've been stressing yourself out to achieve? Rarely are we satisfied even when we do complete a task we feel we should be doing, because right behind it stands a whole squabbling line of them, each as persistent and convincing as the last. A self-perpetuating cycle of perceived inadequacies, effort, perceived shortcomings, and greater effort, there's no winning given this rodent-wheel way of thinking.
- *It drowns out the voice of our intuition.* When preoccupied with what we "should" be doing, it's much more difficult to hear the quieter, less nagging wisdom deep within us. This disregard for our inner knowing further perpetuates the sense that something is missing and keeps us adding more in a futile attempt to satisfy our deepest longings.
- *One size doesn't fit all.* Those boldly dictating the majority of the "shoulds" in our culture (namely advertisers and fear-driven loved ones) offer an extremely narrow context within which to understand ourselves and others. Because each mother is unique, there is no possible way for marketers or our mothers-in-law to paint an accurate picture of us. When we buy into

their stories and priorities anyway, our true selves protest and the gaps grow.

- *Most "should stories" are unchecked.* Chances are that whenever someone suggests you should be a certain way, that story was never checked within them. Rarely does an examined "should story" get passed on to someone else.

- *We miss out on the truest sources of joy and connection.* Burdened with thoughts of what we're not accomplishing, we miss opportunities for impromptu connection, unexpected beauty, and deep presence. "Shoulds" keep us living in the past or future. The present moment has no use for them, as the *now* encompasses only being and doing. The simple thought, "I should be doing something else," blocks our view of the beauty and joy available here and now.

- *It's rooted in history we don't wish to repeat.* "Mothers should stay home and raise their families. ... Women should stay in the kitchen where they belong. ... Mothers should be sedated during labor." Widely-accepted messages just one generation ago, these antiquated "shoulds" gave birth to those being perpetuated today: "Mothers should work outside the home. ... Our homes should stay clean no matter how busy we are. ... Women should be able to handle all that's piled on their plates and still look fresh and unfazed." Deeply-rooted unexamined stories can be especially difficult to untangle ourselves from.

- *"Shoulds" create resentment.* Living according to who we think we should be doesn't feel like freedom but obligation. Over time, this perceived obligation breeds resentment and resistance, which inevitably affect our relationships with others and trust in ourselves.

When motivated by who we think we should be instead of who we really are beneath our stories, the most natural and fluid expression of ourselves is dammed. Over time, this damming creates pressure. Our true self—the part of us that knows it was born to flow freely—begins to push back. We feel frustrated. We feel discontent and disconnected. We feel insatiable and hungry for things that seem just beyond our reach. Society knows this hunger well and feeds it all kinds of empty calories. It tells us to shop more and organize our closets. It says, "You deserve a nicer car," and "Think of all you could buy at zero percent interest." But these promises offer us little relief, like removing a single brick from a dam wall for just a few minutes. Deconstructing our dams is not a one-time endeavor but a lifelong commitment to story examination, truth telling, courage cultivating, and heart healing.

The Mind-Set Shift That Changed Everything

I had no idea what would happen when I started taking bricks out of that dam wall. My wall of security, my wall of certainty, my wall of false empowerment and self-righteousness and fear. What I *did* know was that something was stirring deep within me and pleading—if weakly—for my attention. Like a half-starved barefoot child with sad eyes and outstretched hands, my soul begged me humbly, though with little hope. Having been ignored so many times in the past, it knew better than to expend energy making a scene.

Four babies in, I finally heard it. Though faint and weak, the voice was familiar. My own soul was begging to be nourished and willing to settle for whatever scraps I deemed it worthy of.

Mind you, I see all of this in retrospect. Had you asked me at the time, I'd simply have told you, ashamedly, that I was miserable. That I was so tired, so defeated, and increasingly afraid of what might happen if I continued to hold on so tightly to my crazy-high standards.

It was slowly occurring to me that my well-being *had* to matter. That if I didn't add myself back into the lineup of people whose souls deserved to be fed, my kids were going to look back at their childhood and remember not the handmade dolls and homemade meals but how stressed their mom was while making them. They weren't going to cherish the memories of their tidy, nurturing childhood home but instead beat themselves up in an effort to achieve the impossible, just as I had taught them to. If I didn't begin to care for, honor, and nurture myself, how would they ever learn to care for, honor, and nurture themselves?

My kids needed me to matter to me.

In the weeks and months that followed this realization—as I began to get time away, put much-needed boundaries in place, and prioritize my own basic needs for the first time in years—I unknowingly began rewriting an unconscious agreement that I had made with myself.

The old terms stated that I vowed to do anything to ensure the well-being of my four daughters.

The new agreement had an expanded focus. I would do my best to promote the well-being and wholeness of *five* women.

Five whole women. At long last, *I* was beginning to matter to me too. At long last, my *own* needs stood among my considerations.

Chapter 10

UNMET NEEDS:
A MOTHER'S
GREATEST BURDEN

Only since the Industrial Revolution have most people worked in places away from their homes or been left to raise small children without the help of multiple adults, making for an unsupported life.

—MARTHA BECK

One of my greatest frustrations as a mother (if not *the* greatest) has been the constant management of so many *conflicting* needs and desires. My kids need me (each in different ways), my husband needed me (nearly as much as the kids), the house needs me (the family makes sure of this), my work needs me (my *passions* make sure of this) and of course, my bank accounts need me too. Mixed in among the constantly changing and boldly expressed *needs* all around me are a mess of *desires*, relentless as laundry and just as impossible to ignore.

My motherload, if you will, has felt so heavy through the years that removing my *own* needs and desires from the mix often seemed the only way to stay afloat. Reasoning that I was strong enough to endure, I denied the existence of most of my needs and desires, seeing them as extravagances I didn't have time to consider.

Had you asked me twelve years ago what I needed (before my tipping point), I'd likely have responded (with a convincing smile), "Who, me? Oh, I'm good. I don't need anything." I'd then have changed the subject back to my kids or my projects or whatever the current crisis. Even after I realized that this mind-set was making me miserable, it took a good while for me to quit apologizing for "being a burden," when asking for help or expressing a personal preference.

These oh-so-common stories—that our own needs and desires as mothers (and as women) are less important or worthy than everyone else's, and that we owe the world an apology for taking up space and being human—not only speak of our level 3, self-imposed oppression but they also cultivate exactly the opposite effect that most of us are going for.

Quite simply, when we fail to recognize and honor our own needs and deepest desires, everyone pays.

If I'm not getting enough sleep because the house needs attention, I'm not only saying "the household needs are more important than my well-being," but I'm also likely to be more grouchy with my family on little sleep. If I say yes to yet another engagement when I'm already maxed, I'm not only saying, "coming across as helpful and agreeable is more important than meeting my needs," but I'm also setting myself up for feelings of resentment that tend to have a ripple effect. If I drive all over town so that my children receive the best in extracurricular activities despite the stress it causes me, I'm not only saying to them, "your quality of life is more important than mine," but I'm also sending them messages about what it means to be a mother, a woman, and a caring person. I'm defining my value and worthiness for them.

Still not convinced that your needs matter as much as theirs do? Think of it this way: Every time you deny your own needs for the sake of those around you, you are teaching your daughters how they should expect to be treated (and treat themselves) should they one day become mothers. In the same way, every time you put yourself last, you are modeling the worthiness of mothers for your sons. The very same sons who will grow up to respect and revere their own children's mother ... or not.

We teach people how to treat us, largely based on how we treat ourselves.

Your kids need *you* to matter to *you*. How else will *they* learn to matter to *them*? Here's a simple mantra that's saved me time and again in moments when self-denial seems like the most reasonable route:

Treat yourself as you'd have your children treat themselves.

Adopting this perspective can be a complete game changer. It's also okay if you're not there yet. It takes time to become comfortable admitting that we have needs and also valuing ourselves enough to prioritize meeting those needs. I used to see any and all self-focus as *selfish* and my full investment in others a reflection of my endless generosity. But with every twist and turn in my mothering journey, particularly the uphill climbs and slippery slopes (of which there have been many), it became more obvious that ignoring my needs greatly confuses matters for everyone by implying that I am either superhuman, *sub*-human, or otherwise exempt from the laws of nature.

Denying my needs and desires also:

- Creates unrealistic and entitled expectations in my kids.
- Confuses my partner about his role in our relationship.
- Creates boundary issues with family and friends.

- Cultivates codependency.
- Breeds resentment, disempowerment, and eventual burnout.

Because the fullest expression of our truest selves is no less than a fundamental driving life force, our needs and desires will not go away, no matter how deeply we stuff them. By failing to bring them into the light and examine them for what they really are and instead reacting to the feeling of frustration they generate within us when repressed, we deepen our pain and suffering, behave in ways that are inconsistent with who we truly are, and then feel shame when we're inauthentic. We then blame others for not meeting our needs for us, feel guilty for being reactive, and feel even less worthy of having our needs met!

It's an exhausting, self-perpetuating cycle. Our energy is better spent understanding and communicating our needs rather than resenting others for not anticipating them or reading our minds.

Though selflessness is often praised in our culture, habitually putting the needs of others ahead of our own might be more accurately thought of as an act of self-abandonment or self-betrayal. We may reason that we're merely compromising or that their needs are truly more important (and in specific moments, they really may be). But there's an essential distinction to be made between compromise and self-abandonment, which Caroline Myss articulated beautifully and simply in an interview with Oprah: "In a compromise you don't go away feeling that you've betrayed yourself."[12] The two of them went on to discuss the fact that compromise doesn't feel like it's costing us our power, our psyches, and our souls.

Hiding behind the needs and desires of our children does more than merely distract us—it detaches us from the essence of who we are, compounding our discontentment. Reasoning that we are happiest when others are happy, though noble *sounding*, is also often evidence of codependency. Depending upon the happiness of others and living in such a way that we assume will ensure this happiness places a disproportionate degree of responsibility on us for *their* needs and them for *ours*. This arrangement leads to all kinds of disconnection and, ultimately, dysfunction.

The "Easy" Way

Throughout history, women have been told (and sold) three predominant stories about our needs and desires:

1. They can be satiated through the acquisition of material possessions.
2. They can be conveniently buried beneath the needs and wants of others so that we don't have to feel them day in and day out.
3. We aren't worthy of our deepest desires anyway, so we may as well hedge our bets on a gold-paved afterlife.

The first story is quite clearly the foundation upon which marketers make their millions. The second is a pain management strategy of the disempowered and oppressed; and the third, whatever your take on religious traditions, is a relatively effective way to keep unhappy people hopeful and thus, pacified.

In addition to the stories we're told, many of us learn to put others' needs and desires ahead of our own because it seems so much *easier*.

- It's easier to give in when they beg us beyond set boundaries because we want peace and they'll be quieter quicker.
- It's easier to clean the house frantically before guests arrive than it is to feel ashamed of our mess and judged for the way we live.
- It's easier to keep quiet in a room full of people whose opinions we disagree with than it is to be vulnerable and speak our truth.
- It's easier to build even thicker walls around our hurting hearts than it is to face the fear of deconstructing them.

In many ways, we want to believe others' needs are more important than ours because it saves us the pain of having to face how discontent or disconnected from our truths we really are. Motherhood is a wonderful hiding place when we can't bear to face the truth of our own soul-starvation. Though ignoring our needs may seem to speed up the process of achieving the positive feelings we want, in reality, it slows the process of growth and change necessary for true and lasting inner peace.

Your Unique Needs for Thriving

When I am alone, I feel myself coming alive. Energy pours in from the quiet and beauty all around me and restores my hurried, hungry soul. I receive more from a day alone, in fact, than a week's worth of vacation with my kids. This does not mean that I don't adore my family or enjoy being with them. It just means that silence is my elixir. I did not choose introversion; I was born this way. Resisting this by staying overstimulated, pushing myself to my energetic edges, and habitually sacrificing my well-being for those I love reduces my ability to embody and thus *offer* love in the form of patience, kindness, generosity, compassion, and wholehearted presence.

Alone time is right up there with sufficient sleep and nourishing food and regular exercise when it comes to needs I can't afford to compromise on. If thriving is my goal (and it is), devotion to these needs is essential. Right behind these primary needs are a few that come in a close second. Contemplative conversation, time to create, enlivening my wildness, and time in the woods are needs that I can go a *little* longer without meeting before I feel their absence, but not much.

Devotion to the tending of my needs makes me a better, more whole-feeling person. It's good for me, and it's good for those around me, which, ultimately, means that it's socially responsible.

What I didn't realize early on in my mothering experience is that *my family needs me thriving*. That deep down, just as much as they want me to take them to the mall or make them dinner, they want to see me happy and centered. Valuing my own needs is a gift not only to myself but also to every family member, friend, and individual I interact with.

Chapter 11

MOTHERING OURSELVES BACK TO WHOLENESS

Self-care is never a selfish act—it is simply good stewardship of the only gift I have, the gift I was put on earth to offer to others.

—Parker Palmer

One of the sweetest fantasies I can imagine involves spending a day with all four of my daughters as 2- or 3-year-olds. Just thinking of them giggling and interacting with one another—two blondes, two brunettes, varied in their curiosities and abilities, so young but still so totally *themselves*—brings tears to my eyes.

What about this seems so sweet? None of them was inhibited by anything at that age. Their essence was still pure, untamed, and uninfluenced by the harshness and complexities of life. Their light shone brightly, often cutting through the fog of my confusion and pointing me toward something deep and true and hungry within myself.

I, too, was blessed with a relatively safe-feeling, love-filled childhood. Some of my earliest, sweetest memories include lying in bed at dawn and watching the dance between two chestnut trees outside my upstairs window, walking joyfully and reverently through freshly fallen snow in my moon boots, and "working" dreamily alongside my mom in her garden or my dad in his woodshop. I often played alone in my closet, imagining it to be my own home, and still remember the elation I felt when my parents told me I could run an extension cord and add a lamp to my "living room."

I believe these memories stand out to me because my soul was fully awake and engaged in those moments. The essence of me was tapped into the essence of life, and bliss was mine.

But then I grew up a little and learned that it was weird to play alone in my closet. I started hiding my diary in extra-safe places and feeling funny about my nighttime ritual of getting cozy-warm under the covers before removing my socks so that I could experience the sensual ecstasy of cool sheets on my feet. When I turned 10, I received a radio alarm clock as a birthday present. Pop culture and cool people soon replaced horses and song circles in my fantasy world. I still remember the embarrassment I felt when I realized that no one but me chose their reading glasses based on their undying admiration for their 50-year-old science-loving teacher and their desire to be just like her.

I buried my essence deeper and deeper as I grew up. It felt safer to conform to the ways I "should" behave and do "normal" things that everyone else seemed to enjoy. Over time, I denied much of my true nature, repressing desires and dreams that seemed too big or too impractical or too weird. By the time I hit seventh grade, popularity was all that mattered, and I was willing to do whatever it took to be accepted by those who clearly determined my social fate.

In high school, I became less concerned with being cool and more interested in all things *alternative*. When I became pregnant at 16, however, and realized that the category of "alternative" was a bit too broad and drug-filled to support my new passion as a mother, I settled into a long stretch of *wholesome, natural,* and *handmade.* Feeling closer to my essence than I had in ages, I clung tightly to this self-constructed identity/set of values and created an idealistic, rigid set of rules for myself that demonstrated my commitment to what I believed in.

Most of us can identify a similar progression throughout our lives. We try on one identity after the next until we finally arrive at something that suits us well enough or that allows us to feel relatively successful, relatively accepted, and relatively safe.

The trouble with this progression is that we tend to leave important parts of ourselves behind along the way. Often, not every part of who we are seems to fit into the current phase of life we find ourselves in, so we invest in the sense of self that seems to serve us best at the time and deny or repress the needs, desires, and truths that feel too scary, challenging, painful, or inconvenient to face. It's also common to forget that certain aspects of ourselves ever existed, though we still feel their absence.

The deeper I dove into my identity as a mother, for example, the further I swam away from my quiet, contemplative, wild, sensual, solitude-loving nature. Life as a mom of four young children left little room for introspection or alone time. And because I saw their needs as more important than mine, many soul-draining years passed before I recognized how cut off I was from these essential parts of who I am. My commitment to my maternal self (which revolved around all things natural, wholesome, of the earth, and good for my children) led to the denial of crucial aspects of myself as a *woman.* This eventually led me to misery.

Self-Abandonment

It wasn't until I came across an article by Dr. Margaret Paul about *self-abandonment* that I began to understand the true impact my self-denial had been having on my life. Through Paul's work and by putting her theories to the test, I discovered that by cutting ourselves off from vital aspects of who we are—from our essence and our wholeness—we stress our lives, compromise our relationships, and set ourselves up for resentment, jealousy, anxiety, anger, and a sense of isolation. In the initial article I read, she explains the stress that self-abandonment has on our primary relationships:

> When you abandon yourself emotionally, physically, spiritually, financially, relationally and/or organizationally, you automatically make your partner responsible for you. Once you make another person responsible for your feelings of self-worth and well-being, then you attempt to manipulate that person into loving you, approving of you and giving you what you want. The controlling behavior that results from self-abandonment creates huge relationship problems.[13]

I quickly came to see that it's no different in our relationships with our children. When we self-sacrifice to the point of resentment, we are abandoning our most basic needs and desires. We are abandoning our *inner* child. In doing so, we send the message to that little girl within that she is not worthy of being cared for *by us*, which makes us dependent on *others* to validate our worth and manage our unmet needs. As a result, every time our children misbehave, act insane or bratty in public, reject our authority, have trouble in school, rebel, or engage in self-harming behaviors, our sense of self-worth is on the line because the inner child feels like a failure. This often leads to feelings of embarrassment, shame, isolation, failure, and low self-esteem.

I was deeply impacted by this idea. It was one thing to be hard on myself, but the idea of *abandoning* myself felt unacceptable and less than aligned with my values.

Though self-abandonment is something most people struggle with in some way or another, motherhood is a breeding ground for this insidiously self-destructive behavior. From the time children are born, their needs are intense, relentless, and literally screamed in our faces. Luckily for them (and the human race) we are biologically wired to respond to their needs, even when it means setting aside our own. While our nurturing, self-sacrificial instincts are beautiful and life-preserving, they're also a fast track to burnout, resentment, exhaustion, and destruction, if we're not careful. It's natural to minimize our needs in the interest of the beautiful beings we love, but it's *not* natural that we're raising our children in isolation and that the bulk of their needs are falling on one person instead of a tribe of extended family members and friends. This, and other profoundly affecting gaps within our culture, makes self-awareness and self-nurturing that much more essential. Unfortunately for some of us, it isn't until we're so emotionally or physically wrecked by our self-abandonment that we realize how disconnected from crucial parts of ourselves we really are.

Anything's Better Than a Spinal Tap, Right?

During my baby-having days, the majority of my closest friends were people who both understood and could handle high levels of chaos. In other words, unless you had a mess of kids and more passions than available brain cells with which to pursue them (like me), you'd either be too exhausted or annoyed in our presence to stick around for very long (or for me to want you to).

One friend during this season of my life "got it" and got *me* more than most. A mother of five daughters (yes, that makes nine daughters between us) and as passionate and idealistic as I was, she and I invested fully in our babies. Inspired by deep reverence for motherhood, a desire to give our daughters the most rich and wholesome of childhood experiences, and shared passions for home birth, breastfeeding, and natural everything, we gave and we gave and we gave.

Receiving wasn't something either of us felt particularly comfortable with.

As the years passed, each of us started exhibiting unique signs of burnout (as well as maturation). I put one of mine in public school; she weaned one earlier than she'd planned. I gave up the cloth diapers; she started frequenting drive-throughs on the way home from school. Though invested in our children's thriving, *we* stayed solidly rooted in survival mode. By the time Hunter and I were so fried that we decided to move the family to Mexico, my friend had begun to experience stress-related health problems. It was becoming harder to deny for each of us: something had to give. Self-sacrifice had proven not only unsustainable but also physically and emotionally unhealthy.

A few years ago, while catching up over the phone, my friend told me about several alternative treatments she'd been trying (if somewhat reluctantly), in order to improve her health and feel better. Her doctor had made it clear that if she didn't do something, she'd soon be facing more extreme and invasive options. I'll never forget the way she explained her motivation for change:

"I guess it's better than a spinal tap."

As she spoke the words aloud, we both let out an exhausted, slightly-disturbed, can-you-believe-this-is-our-life kind of half-laugh/half-moan. Giving up this much of ourselves seemed like a good idea when our babies were propped happily on our hips, our breasts expanding in perfect sync with their needs. But somewhere along the way—somewhere between scrubbing soiled couch cushions, wondering where our teenagers were at 1:00 a.m., making birthday muffins and amends in our marriages—we lost ourselves. We abandoned the little girls within us, loving only the little girls around us. We ignored the soft, weak pleas from within, while responding to every demand and insistence outside of us. We gave love endlessly to others but forgot—or never realized to begin with—that we deserved our sweet, maternal love too.

At 42 years old, following a dozen years of deconstructing facades, untangling myself from story after story, and regathering the left-out pieces of myself, I can honestly say that I feel whole again. This reclamation has required stepping out of my comfort zones, braving vulnerability (with strangers and in my most intimate relationships, alike), owning the ways I've hurt others and admitting to all the ways I've abandoned myself. It's required painful truth-telling, letting go of toxic and disempowering relationships, and standing up for my own lovability, needs, and worth. It's required taking more time for me, asking for help, owning, understanding, and healing from my codependency, and learning to be okay with others' disappointment.

Though at times it's hurt like hell and literally brought me to my knees, every bit of the fear and discomfort and heartbreak has been worth it. Like a bird without wings or a tree cut from its roots, I could never be my most powerful, fully-actualized self while disconnected from essential needs, truths, and intuitive knowings. Every wise woman you will ever meet won that wisdom through acts of courage, humility, patience, and perseverance. Every whole woman you will ever meet refused to leave a single stone unturned within her vast inner landscape.

Your Inner Landscape

Imagine for a moment the most beautiful landscape you've ever witnessed. Go there in your mind and feel it in your heart. What does it look like? What does it feel, sound, and smell like? Maybe it glows with morphing mystery where the land meets the sky. Perhaps gently dancing trees reflect their swaying silhouettes on still water. Are there mountaintops lost in clouds, pounding tropical rains, or shimmering dewdrops on a dawn meadow?

A landscape just as stunning, vast, and glorious exists within you. Your inner landscape is every bit as mysterious and no less powerful than the most beautiful outer landscapes that anyone has ever beheld. Just as the outer landscape has the potential for growth, creation, restoration, and healing, so, too, does your inner landscape. And just as any seascape, mountain pass, or old growth forest, your inner land-scape has unique and diverse characteristics.

Some areas are more fluid than others. Some regions are more rigid, sharp, and defined. Within you exist wells of pain and sorrow, deep oceans of compassion, craters of love lost, clouds of passing thoughts, rivers of conscious awareness, and always the potential for unexpected storms.

All the elements of your inner landscape exist in a delicate, resilient, and ever-evolving balance. Every part of who you are is import-ant. Every part of you affects the whole.

Where has your landscape been mistreated? What regions have been neglected or abandoned? Which ones feel scary in their wild-ness? Are the tender shoots and wounded places given extra love and care or ignored out of fear and shame?

A healthy inner ecology is not created by analyzing, criticizing, or judging. It develops naturally when cared for by devoted, loving stew-ards. We are not the oceans of pain, nor the valleys of anxiety, nor the rivers of worry. We are the one tending these beautiful parts; we are the stewards of our inner landscapes. The nurturers, the tenders, the cultivators, the healers. We are the ones we've been waiting for.

We do not gaze upon a landscape outside of us and think, "That purplish hue really ought to be a little more subdued," or "I hate the way that river never stops flowing even for a second." We marvel at the beauty around us. We're blown away by its magnificence. We stand in heart-swelling awe.

Our inner landscapes deserve the same reverence.

Many of us have grown accustomed to hostile inner landscapes. But until we create a loving, gentle, well-tended inner world, our souls will want to stay hidden. Though your soul longs to be seen, and its whole purpose is to shine and guide us with its light, it needs to know that it won't be beaten up or neglected or shamed back into the shad-ows. Only you can create safe inner space for your soul. Your soul longs for *your* love and acceptance more than any other.

Your inner landscape does not need your dissection or categorization or disdain in order to heal and sprout new life. It does not even need your understanding. It needs your awe, your attention. It needs to feel heard and honored and respected.

What are the characteristics of your uniquely beautiful inner landscape? What does it need in order to thrive and flourish again? What has your soul been trying to tell you for years?

No matter what your story has been up until this point—as a woman or as a mother—it is possible to reconnect with your essence and reclaim the fullness of your being. The more comfortable we can become with the ever-changing, usually messy, unpredictable nature of womanhood and motherhood, the better chance we have of reclaiming all the missing pieces of ourselves. You are the only one who's been entrusted with this vital task.

Claim it as your sacred honor.

The Unselfishness of Self-Love

You love your children beautifully. You honor them, encourage them, and learn what makes them tick. You celebrate them, forgive them, and hold them when they're hurt. You nourish, protect, nurture, teach, listen to, cheer, and stand up for them. You are gentle, patient, kind, understanding, and supportive. Of course, you aren't perfect at all these things—and you can't be all these things all the time. Some days, loving them is easier than others, but on the whole, you can't help but love your kids. They mean the world to you.

Let's try a quick experiment. Change the wording in the previous paragraph so that you are speaking about yourself instead of your children:

I love myself beautifully. I honor myself, encourage myself, and learn what makes me tick. I celebrate myself, forgive myself, and hold myself when I'm hurt. I nourish, protect, nurture, teach, listen to, cheer, and stand up for myself. I am gentle, patient, kind, understanding, and supportive to myself.

Does it make sense anymore? Does it apply to you at all?

Our generation of mothers has made incredible strides toward the understanding, honoring, and respecting of children as worthy human beings. Gone are the days (in most social circles, anyway) when a swift whack upside the head following a sassy remark would be affirmed by an observing mother with a "serves 'em right" nod of approval. More likely, judgment would be passed and/or CPS called. And though many mothers are now struggling with how to maintain some semblance of order and authority without physical punishment, across the board, parents and child development experts alike are coming to see the need for greater compassion, empathy, kindness, and tolerance toward growing people of all ages.

But for all the growth in consciousness around what it means to love and care for our children, most of us are still a little clueless when it comes to the hows and whys of loving ourselves. In fact, many of us hardly know what self-love means, much less how to put it into practice. And it's really little wonder.

Consider the messages we received from the time we were young that enforce the notion of loving *others,* while all but ignoring our own needs and desires:

- We were told to share no matter what we actually felt like doing.
- We were told to be nice even when others treated us poorly.
- We were scolded when we expressed a feeling different from those we "should" be having.
- We were told or shown that our emotions were too strong.
- We were rewarded for being selfless or behaving in ways that made us easy to teach and parent.

And while our caregivers may have had pure and loving motives, and many messages we received no doubt helped us conform to safety rules and social norms, we were rarely—if ever—given permission to do the opposite: to express strong feelings, to embrace our fair share, and to be true to ourselves no matter the outcome. Instead, we walked through childhood unconsciously seeking love, acceptance, and security, and behaving in ways we were told would *earn* it.

Truth is, there are many reasons self-love isn't too high on the priority list for most mothers:

- We're biologically wired to care for others, first and foremost.
- Those "others" require a ton of our time and energy, leaving precious little left for us at the end of the day.
- We're taught to think of self-care as a luxury (like having our nails done or spending the day at a spa).
- Self-love wasn't modeled for most of us growing up. Many of our own mothers exhibited self-sacrifice as the rule, dismissing their own needs, even when doing so resulted in anger, dysfunction, martyrdom, and resentment.
- Many subtle and not-so-subtle cultural and familial messages have taught us to equate self-love with selfishness.
- We don't feel worthy of love because we know our own "dark side" and downfalls.
- Some religions and faith communities reinforce the notion that we are wretched and unlovable at the core or that serving others while denying the self is the path to salvation.
- Many of us weren't told or shown that we were lovable when we were young. The voices around us when we were children became our inner voices.
- We fail to measure up to unrealistic cultural and self-imposed standards, which leads us to believe that we're unlovable and unworthy.

- We're constantly fed messages that we must be thin, youthful, and flawless in order to be desirable and therefore, lovable.
- We're ashamed of certain aspects of our stories, which leads to self-loathing.

The definition of self-love makes further sense of why it's such a struggle for so many of us. Here's how Merriam-Webster defines it:

1. conceit
2. regard for one's own happiness or advantage

Dictionary.com makes it seem ever scarier:

1. the instinct by which one's actions are directed to the promotion of one's own welfare or well-being, especially an excessive regard for one's own advantage
2. conceit; vanity
3. narcissism

While promoting our own welfare and regarding our own happiness may sound like good ideas, they hardly seem worth it, given the ever-looming threat of potential conceit, vanity, and narcissism. We all know people who are full of themselves, selfish, self-righteous, image-obsessed, and/or on the narcissistic spectrum, which reaffirms the unfortunate notion that self-love is a dangerous, misguided use of the love within us.

Look up "love" in the dictionary and you'll find nothing about its downsides and risks. We're all well aware of these risks (codependency, heartbreak, obsession, etc.) but we love others anyway, because we know love to be *worth it*. We don't throw the baby out with the bathwater; we simply learn how love works so we know how to do it better.

Self-love is no different. Though it's been misrepresented as a path to self-absorption and selfishness, this unfortunate story reflects only the shadow side of self-love while completely missing the endless goodness and potential it holds. Mysterious, powerful, nourishing, and healing, it's nothing to be feared or avoided or ashamed of, but revered, practiced, and learned about, so that we might learn to do it well and reap its endless benefits.

Remothering Ourselves

My experience of self-love has been profound and profoundly affecting when it comes to my experience of motherhood. I'd even describe it as the number one key to my growth as a woman, my confidence as a mother, my inner peace, and my ability to love others well. But it didn't come easily or quickly to me. For the longest time, I simply didn't get it, and even felt annoyed whenever the idea was mentioned. Its mainstream associations with consumer culture-created self-indulgences were particularly off-putting to me.

As with most mind-set shifts, it took untangling myself from cultural and familial stories before I could taste and benefit from self-love in its purest form. I now have a relationship with myself that feels much like a compassionate, patient mother caring for a child she adores. It's not perfect, but it feels safe, nurturing, and forgiving. My inner world is no longer a hostile, judgment-filled war zone but a peaceful, wholesome home that promotes my continued growth and healing and supports me when I'm down.

My self-relationship was taken to a whole new level when teenage-rearing hit. Thinking back to my own self-destructive choices and habits at their age, it quickly became obvious that my kids *needed* me to love myself. The less I was able to protect them from the world and their limited understanding of it, the more important it's been that they learn to care for *them*selves. The more complex their struggles become, the more they need me to lead by example, especially given that our culture is so *mis*leading.

Simply put, children learn how to love others by watching us love others, but they learn to love themselves by watching us love ourselves. When we treat ourselves as we'd have our children treat themselves, everyone wins.

My Inner Counsel

Over the years I've developed a beautiful relationship with my inner 9-year-old, my inner 17-year-old, and my inner 80-year-old. These girls and women are my inner counsel. I consult them when making decisions, tune into them and ask for their guidance when something in my life feels "off," and ask them for help when my 42-year-old self isn't feeling strong or centered or able to see things clearly.

My 9-year-old is especially good at reminding me how much richness there is to be found in my aloneness. She knows that in order to be able to have fun with someone, a felt sense of safety is key. She is all about lightness and playfulness and wonder over the smallest things.

My 17-year-old is especially good at idealistic dreaming and exploring wildness. She reminds me to dream bigger and play harder and gives me loads of permission and encouragement to explore and expand my sensual and sexual nature. She doesn't shy away from the darker aspects of life, is endlessly curious, and is okay with taking risks.

My inner 80-year-old is wise and serene and wholehearted. She reminds me to live boldly and bravely and not take shit from anyone. She encourages me to shake things off quickly and not waste time on people and circumstances too small for me. She also gets after me when I don't exercise or eat well or sleep enough. I can almost hear her as I'm resisting my morning run, "Ummm, hello. What about me? What is your choice not to workout doing to *me*?"

I first had to repair my relationship with the younger versions of me before they trusted that I *wanted* a relationship with them. Each felt abandoned and hurt by choices I've made throughout my life.

My inner 17-year-old felt resentful and slighted of her freedom for years. The year I became a mother was also the year I swapped my newly emerging freedom for hyper-responsibility. In a powerful visualization guided by my counselor a few years ago, I met and had a conversation with her (my 17-year-old self) in which we each realized we actually needed and deeply admired one another. Toward the end of our tender, tearful meeting, we exchanged gifts. She gave me back the treasures of lightness and fun that I'd lost so many years ago, and I promised to keep her safe as she explores her wildness. That encounter changed my life. It continues to enrich my days in exciting, unexpected, and profoundly beautiful ways.

My inner 9-year-old helped me out of my life-draining marriage. As I was beginning to contemplate separation from my husband, I found a photo of myself at age 9 and asked her: What are you disappointed about that I'm not doing with our life? What are you sad about that I *am* doing?

Her answers were clear, painful, and liberating to hear. She was disappointed that I wasn't singing more (harmonizing, specifically). I quickly joined our local community choir and cried my way through that first season as the starved-for-song little girl within realized I wasn't going to ignore her desires any longer. She was sad that I was settling for love that didn't represent the sweet, soul-nourishing, safe-feeling connection she dreamed we would one day have. I committed to reorienting toward love in such a way that honored her need for safety and sweetness and playfulness and nourishment. She reminded me that true love feels life-giving and self-expanding, not exhausting and soul-constricting. (My ex-husband felt exhausted by me, too, by the way. We make much better friends and co-parents than we did life partners.)

More recently—feeling beautifully remothered—I've recognized that I also need re*fathering*. Having cultivated loads of self-love and self-compassion and self-tenderness, I'm now working on developing greater self-protection, assertiveness, and a stronger "hell no." Developing these more masculine qualities within myself is helping me escape the burden of over-giving, over-caretaking, and saying yes from a place of compassion for others at the expense of my own well-being.

True self-love isn't about feeding the ego. It's about nurturing the parts of ourselves that the ego has been mistreating. We do this by getting still, asking difficult questions, and listening deeper for answers. We do this by getting the support we need in the form of therapists and counselors and coaches and support groups. We do this by realizing that where we are today—however painful or messy our lives may feel—is exactly the right place from which to grow lives we feel proud of, nourished by, and excited to share with others who are also on the path of growth and healing. We do this through soul work.

Chapter 12

SOUL FIRE STEWARDSHIP

Find out who you are and be that person. That's what your soul was put on this Earth to be. Find that truth, live that truth, and everything else will come.

—Ellen DeGeneres

The Christmas holiday season is particularly fascinating (and historically frustrating) to me. On the one hand, my body, mind, and soul are eager to draw inward, slow down, cozy up, and—like the trees and the bears and all sensible beings—allow myself a time of rest and rejuvenation. On the other hand, nearly all of society, my family, and my conditioning are encouraging me to speed up, get more done, and focus on things that don't allow for much introspection or stillness.

It occurred to me a few years back that late November/early December marks the beginning of a month-long power struggle between my soul and my ego. The capitalism-crazed culture around me appeals to my stimulation, productivity, and perfectionism-craving ego, while my soul longs for sweet serenity.

As a way of supporting my soul during this time and focusing on what matters most to me, I decided to proclaim this season, *The Season of the Soul* and commit to my soul's care and keeping as if it were my job, my #1 responsibility.

This looks like slowing down, saying no, getting outside, breathing deeply, checking the stories that I've created around what I should or have to be doing, limiting (or eliminating) my time with people who drain my energy, taking naps, asking for help, letting things go, starting a new holiday tradition (and focusing on those that inspire me most), simplifying, lighting candles often (to bring light into the ever-darkening days), celebrating solstice, and anything else that my soul seems to be asking me for in the way of nurturance and/or expression.

I become radically attuned to my soul during this season, which strengthens its presence within me for the rest of the year.

I believe we can all benefit from Seasons of the Soul, and not just during the holidays. Whether postpartum, during a challenging relationship reconstruction, amidst a health crisis, or when we're engaged in intense family of origin or ancestral healing work, increased, intentional focus on the soul can bring great meaning and nourishment to our lives and support for our physical, emotional, and spiritual healing.

As a *daily* practice for tuning into the needs, desires, and qualities of my soul, I turn to *soul fire stewardship*. Few practices cut through the madness of motherhood (and everything else) and bring me back to what matters most to me more quickly than tending my soul fire.

Soul Fire

The way I see it, within each of us exists a metaphorical fire that is either well-tended, burning steadily, and benefiting us (and all those who come near us) or a barely-glowing bank of coals in need of our attention. Once we recognize and begin to feel the presence of this fire within, we can begin to orient and organize our lives in ways that ensure its tending and protection. The idea is that we might become skilled and dedicated *soul fire stewards*. In doing so, we not only tap into our fullest potential and deepest joy but we also set ourselves up to be powerful agents for change and instruments for cultural healing.

Soul fire expresses itself in many forms. The essence of our aliveness, it sometimes feels warming and comforting and other times painful and infuriating. Here are some of the manifestations of this powerful force within:

1. Rage—Think back to a time when you felt enraged over an injustice that you either witnessed, heard about, or were personally affected by. Anytime we feel the fury of unjust, cruel, oppressive, or otherwise dishonoring behaviors or circumstances, our soul fire is burning brightly.

2. Passion and Inspiration—Often, when a sense of passion is awakened or stirred within us, the flames of our soul fire are being fanned. This passion could be the result of creating, engaging sensually or sexually, knowing deep in our bones what we are here on this planet to do, witnessing good work in the world that causes us to want to take a greater stand, fighting for a cause we feel strongly about, or anything else that builds heat within.

3. Tenderheartedness—We're feeling the warmth of our soul fire every time we experience tenderhearted love, sadness, grief, or joy. That ache is a beautiful thing, however painful or heart-wrenching it may feel, as it means that our soul fire is aglow.

4. Beauty—The recognition of and basking in beauty of all kinds is some of my favorite soul fire fuel, given that it's always available and requires nothing more than increased receptivity in order to be utilized.

5. Self-Honoring—Every time we make a self-respecting, self-loving choice, we are strengthening our capacity for and commitment to soul fire stewardship. By chipping away at habitual patterns of self-abandonment, caretaking, and putting the needs and desires of others ahead of our own, we are saying, "My soul fire is *worthy* of tending." When our own soul fire is bright and perpetually cared for, we have the capacity to support others from a generous place rather than from a place of depletion and/or resentment. Our soul fire also illuminates the places where stronger boundaries are needed.

6. Courage—When we act with courage, we're essentially protecting and/or standing up for the fire within us. Acting with courage is a way of demonstrating that we believe our soul fires to be worthy of protecting and that we are willing to endure some discomfort in order to guard and encourage the growth of something near and dear to us.

Rage, passion, tenderheartedness, beauty, courage, and self-honoring behaviors are all things to pay particular attention to as we commit to soul fire stewardship. Connection, presence, stillness, and a felt sense of freedom can also help us move closer to the end goal of a steadily-burning, revered fire within.

It's equally essential to recognize the many ways that our soul fire can be compromised. Here are some of the circumstances and phenomenon we must become familiar with as soul fire stewards:

1. Dampening—When we're feeling defeated, deflated, or deeply disappointed, it is as if our soul fire is being dampened. We might feel that we're being affected by a gentle rain or raging storm (which may be annoying to fire tenders, but both are natural, unavoidable, and even healthy occurrences), that we're being doused by a bucket of water (when we're feeling

disrespected by or taken advantage of by a loved one, etc.), or that our soul fire has been blasted by a high-pressure water hose, such as during times or seasons of trauma or high stress. We may eventually realize the need to change our life circumstances so that the hard work we've done to build and maintain our soul fires is not consistently being *undone* and our energies exhausted through constant rebuilding from wet, cold coals.

2. Fuel Shortages—Fuel shortages are common during times of our lives when we're spending so much time tending to the needs and desires of others that we neglect our own fuel supply. They can also occur when our lives feel more stressful and obligatory than inspiring and nourishing.

3. Kindling Fires—Sometimes, such as when we realize the importance of self-care but still don't prioritize much time for it, we might realize that we are feeding our soul fires mere kindling, over and over again. It may have been so long since we put a log on our fire that we've forgotten what it feels like to be warmed by a more substantial, sustaining source.

4. Poor Fire-Tending Skills—Many of us have simply never been taught how to tend our fires well. In fact, poor soul fire-tending skills may be the norm in the lives of our friends and families, making our own desire for something different challenging to imagine, much less to implement.

5. Coal Thieves—Coal thieves are those people in our lives who are so out of touch with their own soul fires that they feel the need to steal glowing coals from others. Such people desperately crave the light and warmth they see and feel emanating from within those of us with well-tended fires, but often don't feel worthy of such warmth from within, so they steal rather than maintain and grow fires of their own.

6. Wildfires—During times of drought, when our soul fires have been neglected and our inner landscapes feel dry and brittle,

we become susceptible to wildfires. Lashing out and burning bridges, engaging in self- and connection-destructive behaviors can be signs that our soul fire is burning uncontrollably.

7. Flare Ups + Diversions—Sometimes we meet someone who causes our soul fire to blaze out of control. This is common when we feel seen or heard after a stretch of feeling invisible or devalued, our sensuality is awakened for the first time in a long time, or we feel intoxicated by a powerful spiritual leader. It's important to recognize that not all soul fire flare-ups are created equal. Some are healthy and sustaining and others are more like gasoline: dangerous, quick to burn away, and likely to cause us pain.

8. Soul-Starving Heat Sources—Our egos aren't into fire tending. In fact, they are experts at convincing us that any old electric plug-in heater will do. While it's true that we can be warmed by "electric heaters" (constant distractions, overeating, numbing, substance use, etc.), they're hardly a substitute for a well-tended, slow burning flame.

A well-tended soul fire can provide us with the strength, warmth, and light we need to affect the world in powerful ways. You can feel it when you're in the presence of someone who tends their fire well. It's hard to look away. It's hard *not* to be bettered by their presence in your life. Ideally, we would be surrounded by those who are committed to soul fire stewardship, themselves. That way, everyone benefits from one another's light and warmth and inner strength without depleting one another (or being depleted).

Modeling soul fire stewardship for our children is a gift that's likely to warm their hearts and light their paths long after we are gone.

Chapter 13

SURRENDERING
TO THIS SEASON

The psyches and souls of women also have their own cycles
and seasons of doing and solitude, running and staying, being
involved and being removed, questing and resting, creating and
incubating, being of the world and returning to the soul-place.

—CLARISSA PINKOLA ESTÉS

I am currently sitting in my favorite tea shop, near a wide-open window, on a blossom-scented late-spring morning. All my immediate
family members are either in school or working, and the day is
mine for writing and dreaming and tea-sipping. I feel deeply content,
and joy is my date for tea.

I can honestly say that I am thriving.

I could not have written those words five years ago. The year my
marriage was being held together by twice-a-week couples therapy and
brokenhearted prayers of surrender. The year my heart officially grew
too large for the walls I'd once built to hide it and trembled, naked and

vulnerable with the newness of constant exposure. The year it became excruciatingly clear that I could no longer protect my girls from the world's harshness and that the majority of their influences were now beyond my control. The year I awakened to my own worthiness and lovability on a whole new level and began to hold space for myself and my process in gentle, nourishing ways.

The difference between the reality I'm currently living and the one I just described feels like the difference between midsummer and the dead of winter. Though I am the same person, with the same family, in the same town, and on the same path of growth and discovery, the seasons have changed, resulting in a totally different-feeling inner landscape.

This 180-degree shift has happened to me time and again throughout my life—so many times, in fact, that I'm finally beginning to trust the turn of the seasons. I now see as much value and beauty in the winter as I do the springtime, however challenging it can feel to endure extended stretches of dormancy and cold. I've learned that the more I lean into the season I'm in, as opposed to resisting and fearing it, the more potential I have to receive its unique and plentiful gifts.

Whatever season I am meant to cycle through next will no doubt feel different than this one. We can never be sure when our life circumstances will shift radically or what the cumulative changes that have already taken place will bring to fruition. This used to cause me a great deal of sadness. I didn't want my babies to grow up. I didn't want to be done nursing forever. It pained me when someone corrected my last-born's sweetly mispronounced words (which I can no longer remember), and when she didn't want to play soccer anymore (I didn't raise a single soccer lover. How did that happen?). I tried desperately to hold onto those sweetest of moments, but no matter how tightly, stubbornly, and *lovingly* I clenched my fists, they still slipped away. The truth is, everything I've ever held tightly has eventually wriggled loose and demanded freedom, including my stubborn resistance to change.

Several months ago, I attended a small business owner meet-and-greet with the hopes of expanding my local community of women entrepreneurs. A web designer and I hit it off quickly, connecting over the unique struggles of balancing small, home-based businesses with the needs of our families and households. She, too, had once given the whole of herself to her family and was now carving out space for new expressions of herself to emerge. She summed up the resulting, inevitable priority shifts in a way that I understood completely: "I used to make my own laundry soap and hang dry our clothes. Now I'm like, 'Who wants a corn dog?'"

I, too, have been in what I've come to think of as a Trader Joe's season of my life, meaning that I make decisions largely based on what's most easily accessible and affordable with the least amount of compromise to my convictions. I can get in and out of that store with fruit and nuts for lunches, chicken breasts free of hormones, low-impact toilet paper, and my favorite ginger tea in under five minutes. There are plenty of organic options, though not too many options in any category, which saves me from having to make that many more decisions. The cashiers are friendly, the prices right, and there are no magazines pushing pop culture and distorted body consciousness on my kids. Do I love their produce selection? Nope. Am I grateful for the option of premade kale salads on the craziest of school nights? Totally.

Another change of seasons is coming. I can feel it. I still frequent Trader Joe's, but I also have a garden again for the first time in seven years. I have houseplants *that are actually thriving,* I've dedicated a corner of my kitchen to my ferments, and there's no telling where my work and relationships will lead me. I have no doubt that next year will bring heartbreak and elation, troubles and treasures, challenges and rich rewards.

One of the primary reasons I'm now thriving is because I've become more comfortable with paradox. My sense of self is no longer precariously perched on the identity of super invested stay-at-home mom, nor is it dependent on escaping domesticity in hopes for a thriving career. I've finally given myself permission to be so much more than any one too-small-for-me label.

I've finally embraced both/and.

Both/And

Part of reclaiming and nurturing our felt sense of wholeness is recognizing that there is so much more to each of us than we've been led to believe. Women are complex and multi-dimensional beings. We are darkness and light, terrified and brave, plain and fancy, certain and uncertain all at once. Mothers are an expanded expression of womanhood. We are sacred passageways, nurturers of tender new life, and committed to radical love no matter the cost.

But because we live in a world that celebrates sameness and tidiness and easily explicable (and controllable) categories, most of us are confused by our own complex and seemingly-conflicting nature.

We don't expect a mother wolf to hunt fiercely *or* tend gently to her cubs. She is both fierce and gentle. We don't fault flowers for closing up at night and unfurling during the day or trees for shedding their leaves in one season and blooming in another. They get to be complex. They're allowed to be different one day from the next, one season after the next, and at every stage of their growth.

We, too, need room to grow and change and change our minds. Our ever-evolving nature is something to be celebrated, not ashamed of.

We can be so ready for the kids to go back to school by early August and crave summertime again come March.

We can appreciate our lives as stay-at-home moms and still fantasize about working for pay and without distractions.

We can be brought to tears by the sweetness of nursing our babies and dream of the day when our bodily fluids will again serve only us.

We can parent from a seemingly bottomless well of empathy and understanding one day and feel *so over it all* the next.

We can want more freedom *and* deeply grieve their growing up in the same breath.

Though our richness and mystery are part of what makes us so powerful, many of us are so disconnected from and ashamed of the more sensitive, emotional, and "fickle" ways we're wired that we squander our strength and give away our power. We agree with the limiting stories being told about and for us.

Marianne Williamson explains why in *A Woman's Worth*:

> The world is currently set up according to masculine models of thought and structure, and has been for thousands of years. Aggression, force, domination, and control have been at the heart of our social agreements. Organization, technology, and rational analysis have been the order of this very long day. During this time, the feminine principles of nonviolence and surrender and the values of intuition, nurturing, and healing were pushed aside. We forgot the power of tender touch. Slowly but surely, generation after generation, over thousands of years, the feminine was made to seem ridiculous. She was debased in men as well as in women, all of us risking shame to relate to her. We could know her in bed, and she was good with children. But other than that, she didn't belong here. She wasn't silenced, just invalidated. She could still speak, but she wouldn't be heard. ... No one will listen to us until we listen to ourselves. The Goddess awakens in our hearts before she awakens in the world.[14]

We may look around for examples of self-honoring, motherhood-revering women and find few, if any. This is because we, ourselves, have forgotten our feminine essence, our inherent worth and purpose and strength. To this, Williamson says:

Forget looking for earthly role models, because there aren't many; and even when we do find them, they live their own lives and not ours. We must look instead inside ourselves. The Goddess doesn't enter us from the outside. She emerges from deep within. She is not held back by what happened in the past. She is conceived in consciousness, born in love, and nurtured by higher thinking. She is integrity and value, created and sustained by the hard work of personal growth and the discipline of a life lived actively in hope.[15]

This journey within is not always an easy one. Gathering the pieces of ourselves back together and healing from the wounds of cultural, familial, and self-disrespect take time. It requires that we get still and learn to be with our pain. That we embrace discomfort and welcome vulnerability. That we heal our childhood wounds and traumas. That we get good at both swimming upstream and knowing when to surrender and trust the flow.

More than anything, we need community. We need connection. We need sisterhood to help us weed toxic narratives from their roots and plant seeds of a new narrative; one based in our inherent worthiness, utter importance, and rightful position of power.

Chapter 14

REVILLAGING

The things we need most are the things we have become
most afraid of, such as adventure, intimacy, and authentic
communication. We avert our eyes and stick to comfortable
topics. We hold it as a virtue to be private, to be discreet, so
that no one sees our dirty laundry. We are uncomfortable
with intimacy and connection, which are among the greatest
of our unmet needs today. To be truly seen and heard, to be
truly known, is a deep human need. Our hunger for it is so
omnipresent, so much a part of our life experience, that we no
more know what it is missing than a fish knows it is wet. We
need more intimacy than nearly anyone considers normal.

—CHARLES EISENSTEIN

I haven't always felt supported and held and treasured by other
women like I do now. I haven't always felt that I belonged.

Until half a dozen years ago, in fact, I kept a "safe" distance
from the more vulnerable ways of connecting with women, mothers

and non-mothers alike. Sure, we'd swap childcare and empathize about the chaos of raising kids and the challenges of marriage. Occasionally, I'd even ask for help when life felt especially hard.

But for a long time, I kept my heart guarded. It simply felt too risky to open up about how I really felt, explore what I really needed, or share what I dreamed of beyond the more practical, everyday realms of motherhood and domesticity. I now realize that in my effort to stay safe, I was actually starving my soul.

Thankfully, my life looks and feels radically different (and so much richer) today. I cry on the shoulders of my girlfriends unashamedly, share my heart's deepest pain and longings, and explore the vulnerable, tender places within me *all the time.*

I don't actually know how I would have survived the past five years of my life without this depth of connection. I now realize that it's not actually possible to be my best, most empowered, most fulfilled self without these rich, nourishing, and nurturing relationships.

Safe, soulful sisterhood is the foundation of my well-being. It's the log on my soul fire that burns most slowly, steadily, and brightly.

How did I make the leap? How did I begin connecting more deeply and opening up to other women? In small, courageous, sometimes uncomfortable steps ...

I joined a knitting group, where rich, nurturing conversation was the norm.

I joined a rowing team and made sure to connect with women who interested me.

I started taking African dance classes and pushed through the utter discomfort I felt in the beginning.

I went on my first retreat and practiced being vulnerable with people I may or may never see again.

I dared to share my stories and heart with those who showed up for me consistently, and I eventually learned that many women *could* be trusted.

Every time I did something courageous, my life got a little richer. I soon learned that vulnerability served a very important purpose for me. It was the *gateway* into the life I really wanted.

Ideally, we would all be able to step out our front door, wander down the road, and have tea with our choice of amazing, trustworthy, lifelong friends. I do believe we're wired for village life. In fact, I believe that in the absence of the village, mothers struggle more than anyone else. Given the hundreds of thousands of people who read and shared my most popular blog post to date (titled, naturally, *In the Absence of the Village, Mothers Struggle Most*), it seems that I'm not the only one feeling this way. As I see it, mothers are collectively mourning the loss of the village without even realizing it. The epidemic of anxiety and depression among us is, in large part, evidence of our widespread, unacknowledged maternal grief.

We must begin to name and feel this grief. We must honor our loss in order to transmute our pain into fuel for our mobilization and rising. I believe there's a place in this process for *all* the messy feelings, including the childlike, exhausted proclamations of unfairness and rage over the injustice of having to create our own support structures at a time of life when we're meant to be held within already-existing communities. It *isn't* fair. It's tragically, maddeningly unfair the way things are currently set up for us. Sob furiously into your pillow, scream-sing wildly in your car, or go into the woods and pour out your hurting heart to the grandmother trees. Feeling angry over injustice is essential. Do what you need to do to honor the pain and loss.

Then, once you've allowed grief to soften you a bit, make a commitment to creating a new way. Decide to be a changemaker, not a victim, and join forces with those of us committed (as Charles Eisenstein describes it), to creating The More Beautiful World Our Hearts Know Is Possible.

Though our culture is not currently set up to support rich, nourishing connections between us, we are nonetheless worthy of the connection and belonging we crave. Each of us must make a choice about whether we will perpetuate the old stories and suffer in isolation or reclaim the life-giving birthright of belonging. How? By examining one outdated, soul-fire dampening story at a time.

The hard truth is that most of us will never know what it's like to raise children in an actual village, but *that's okay*. That's not what this generation is about. This generation is about waking up to who we really are and what we really want and then resetting society's sails accordingly. Revillaging starts with creating a village mind-set and restructuring our lives in ways that honor our individual gifts and limitations, meet our universal need for true belonging, and feed our deep desire for rich, authentic, everyday connection.

The Myth of Independence

One story that's wreaking havoc on nearly every aspect of our culture is what I like to call The Myth of Independence. This is no child's fairy tale. This one's a super story, and it's affecting us all in insidious, confusing, and deeply damaging ways. Both overtly and through subtle suggestion, we've been immersed in its substories since we were born. Here are a few examples:

- Independence equals strength and power.
- Needing people makes you weak.
- Relying on people means you're not self-reliant.
- Relying on others makes you burdensome.
- It's shameful to admit to needing or wanting connection with others.
- We need to watch out for #1 because people can't be trusted.
- Daring to be vulnerable with others is a quick way to get hurt and be rejected.

Creating the communities and connections we crave starts with recognizing the presence and power of The Myth of Independence in our lives. It requires that we squint our eyes best we can and look for the ways we perpetuate this myth in our thoughts and everyday choices.

It may feel scary to imagine letting go of this myth and its many substories. We've all been hurt (at some point or repeatedly) when we've dared to lean on others or attempted to cultivate the connections we crave. More often than not, however, the degree of threat we perceive is disproportionate to the presence of actual danger to our well-being. Most of our fears are rooted in unexamined pain, trauma, and coping strategies we've been relying on since we were first hurt, rejected, or misunderstood as kids. These are things we can work with. These are wounds we can heal from.

It takes courage to tell truer, more life-giving stories. The stakes may feel high at times, but the rewards can be truly life-changing and culture-healing.

Our task is not to destroy the entire Myth of Independence at once, but to loosen our entanglement in cultural narratives that no longer serve us and continue examining our stories as a lifelong commitment. When we poke holes in our adopted stories, the light of truth and joys of *inter*dependence can begin to shine through them.

Interdependence, or mutual reliance, is our true human nature. Healthy interdependence is one of our deepest, most universal, and most misunderstood needs/desires as humans. We long to belong, to be an integral part of something meaningful, supportive, life-giving, co-inspired, co-created, and healing, however terrifying it feels to admit this need to ourselves.

Interdependence, or Interbeing as Eisenstein calls it, is where it's at. In his hope-inspiring book, *The More Beautiful World Our Hearts Know Is Possible*, he writes that, "the state of interbeing is a vulnerable state. It is the vulnerability of the naive altruist, of the trusting lover, of the unguarded sharer. To enter it, one must leave behind the seeming shelter of a control-based life, protected by walls of cynicism, judgment, and blame."[16]

In other words, to enter into our truest, most authentic and interconnected way of being in the world, we must deconstruct our walls and learn to trust one another again.

Reclaiming Trust

Jon Young, a leader in the field of nature-based community building for more than thirty years, once said, "The biggest obstacle to creating culture for our children is that the adults no longer trust one another."[17]

I couldn't agree more with this statement. The breakdown of social trust within our culture can be linked to dozens of factors, many of which can feel daunting to imagine changing. Here are just a few:

- The absence of rich, dynamic local communities and neighborhoods.
- Car culture, which keeps us moving fast and cut off from one another.
- Fear mongering in the news.
- Climate control, which keeps people indoors and less interactive with neighbors.
- Economic inequality.
- Technological advancements, which have us feeling less dependent on one another and more dependent on devices.

Robert Putnam, author of *Bowling Alone,* has been studying the decline of trust in the US for nearly two decades. He attributes much of this decline to the fact that people no longer join social organizations such as bowling leagues and Elks lodges, choosing instead to stay in and watch TV.

Much social trust and connection has also been lost in the modernization of our homemaking practices and food production. While our time has been freed up, and a tremendous burden lifted (particularly from the shoulders of women), we no longer visit with one another while washing clothes in the creek, bring in and preserve the crops together, or visit on our porches to keep cool on a hot summer evening. It takes living everyday life together to build trust. Without these day-to-day experiences built-in out of necessity, we must get creative, be intentional, and connect *courageously*.

The first step is to recognize how cornerstone trust is to community building.

The next step is to begin building—or *re*building—our trust muscle. Essential to this is the recognition that some conditions and people help us feel safer than others. This is especially important early on in the trust building process or during particularly vulnerable feeling stretches of time (such as during the postpartum period, when we've recently moved to a new town, or following a divorce).

Think of it like this ... When planting or transplanting a seedling or young plant, we don't put it in the full sun, forget to water it, and expect it to thrive; we keep it close and protect it as it becomes established and acclimates to its new surroundings.

It is much the same when building or rebuilding trust. Some conditions and/or personalities are too harsh and/or triggering to us. They touch our traumas in such a way that keeps us closed off as an instinctive means of survival. Others help us to unfurl, grow, and eventually thrive.

Not everyone is worthy of holding our hearts or shaping our lives. Some community members are meant to support us occasionally and in specific ways, while a small handful of others will end up in our innermost circles. Trust grows slowly, one rich, healthy, nourishing interaction at a time.

It's essential that we be discerning and self-honoring as we learn who we can trust and how deeply we're meant to connect within each relationship we cultivate. This requires that we develop *self*-trust and strengthen our intuition.

Self-Trust

Trusting in others is only part of the equation. We must also cultivate greater self-trust in order to connect more intimately and nourishingly with others. When we don't fully trust ourselves to make decisions in our own best interest or in accordance with our values, we're less likely to connect with others wholeheartedly, courageously, and in healthy ways.

Here are some of the reasons we may not trust ourselves:

- As a culture, we've become reliant on "experts" (and Google) for the answers we seek.
- Historically, we've made choices that didn't serve us well or that weren't aligned with our own integrity.
- We were raised by parents who told us what to do and how to do it, so we didn't develop our self-trust muscle to begin with.
- Women's intuition is not revered nor encouraged as a source of wisdom in our society.
- We've not held healthy boundaries with people who've repeatedly treated us poorly.
- We carry unprocessed, unresolved traumas that keep our nervous systems from relaxing enough to move through and overcome our fears.

Building and restoring self-trust requires making decisions in our best interests, taking good care of ourselves (just as we do other people we love), getting the support we need to heal, setting and holding healthy boundaries, learning when to go within for answers instead of consulting others, and choosing the path of growth over and over again, even when doing so feels foreign and scary.

We must reassure the child within that we will take care of her now. The better and more consistently we care for her, the more quickly self-trust is rebuilt.

If trust building is a cornerstone "how" of community building, then our need for a felt sense of belonging is the "why."

We all long to belong to something greater than ourselves. We're biologically wired for connection, and whether we realize it or not, most every stressor we feel in modern-day culture ties into our lack of belonging within a close-knit community.

A true, felt sense of belonging, however, requires that we simultaneously learn to belong to ourselves more fully. Brené Brown puts it this way:

> Stop walking through the world looking for confirmation that you don't belong. You will always find it because you've made that your mission. Stop scouring people's faces for evidence that you're not enough. You will always find it because you've made that your goal. True belonging and self-worth are not goods; we don't negotiate their value with the world. The truth about who we are lives in our hearts. Our call to courage is to protect our wild heart against constant evaluation, especially our own. No one belongs here more than you.[18]

Simply put, until we develop a healthy self-relationship, no amount of belonging will satiate our deepest hungers. Just as self-trust must be developed in order for trust in others to become second nature, we must also learn to belong to ourselves before we'll feel that we belong anywhere else.

Connecting YOUR Way

For years in my early adulthood, I thought I wanted to be a hermit and spend my days holed up in the woods somewhere, writing and daydreaming and feeling one with the natural world. So I tried it for three years. Turns out that I feel incredibly isolated and disconnected under these circumstances. The most content and inspired I've ever felt, ironically, was when I lived downtown in a small, walkable colonial Mexican city.

I now realize that I *love* having people around me; I simply need to limit my interactions and make sure I'm getting plenty of alone time. My favorite ways to be with people are through dancing, singing, ceremony and ritual, storytelling, contemplative conversations, and intimate gatherings of people who are willing to connect with open hearts. I also love working in tea houses and coffee shops with my headphones on. I feel inspired having people around me, even when I'm not directly interacting with them.

Many of us feel obligated to interact with people in ways that feel completely draining to us. There are few things I dislike more, for example, than small talking at a bar or staying up late for way-too-loud live music. Give me an outdoor camping festival, however, and I will dance my heart out into the wee hours of the morning. PTO at my kids' school? Not so much. Chaperoning for school campout? Totally. It's taken trial and error to come to these realizations. The important thing is to engage, then course correct as you learn about your preferences and needs.

Whether it's a knitting group, dance troupe, church, kayaking club, or homeschool collective, commit to growing community around one area of your life that enlivens you or fills a need. Do you need more fun? Are you hungry for soulful connections or deep conversations? Is there a passion you've set aside or hobby you've been meaning to pursue?

Though it's tempting to fill our lives to the brim with commitments that help us feel like good moms or dedicated community members, motivation based on "shoulds" further disempowers and disconnects us. No one is served when we invest in ways that deplete us. Making a habit of this only leads to inauthentic relating, resentment, and eventual burnout. Remedying this all-too-common overcommitment issue requires that we revisit the notion of trust. The more we come to trust that other good people with big hearts are doing their parts in making the world a better place, and the more fully we can live into our own unique purposes, the less overwhelmed and drained we'll feel.

Courageous, Creative Connections

Most of the connections we make day in and day out are relatively *easy* connections, based on the way we've grown accustomed to interacting with others. We smile at someone we pass in a parking lot, make small talk with the grocery checker, text with our sister or mom, and meet a girlfriend for coffee, but rarely do we deviate much from the kinds of connections we're most comfortable with. Even suboptimal connections, such as arguments with our partner or power struggles with our kids, are at least familiar.

Building rich, supportive community for ourselves, however, requires that we interact more courageously and creatively than most of us are accustomed to.

Courageous connections vary greatly from one interaction to the next. The one thing they have in common is that they feel expansive (they make you bigger, not smaller) and vulnerable (i.e., a little scary).

Here are a few examples:

- Approaching someone you don't know and offering to help them.
- Paying someone a compliment, not just for their cute shoes or beautiful hair but also for an act of kindness or generosity you witnessed.
- Taking initiative and making plans to see someone again, rather than simply swapping numbers.

- Reaching out to someone you admire or would like to explore friendship with.
- Asking for help or accepting help when it's offered.
- Knocking on the doors of your neighbors to introduce yourself.
- Hosting a neighborhood potluck, whether you know the neighbors or not.
- Inviting a friend over, last-minute, no matter the state of your house.
- Volunteering for an organization, club, or class that both excites you and makes you a little nervous.
- Organizing a childcare or meal swap.
- Hosting a book club or starting a knitting group.
- Starting a conversation with someone who seems different than you in one way or another, someone you would usually shy away from.

Just a decade ago, these types of connections were the norm rather than the exception. Now that smartphones and social media provide us with so many ways of staying virtually "connected," in-person interactions often feel foreign and scary. That "muscle" has already atrophied in many of us.

Creativity is key to reversing this tragic trend. We've got to use what we have to create something better. One example of this is my yearlong virtual women's circles called MotherWorthy. Though virtual circles can be seen as suboptimal, this format is proving surprisingly helpful and effective for the dozens of busy mothers who participate every year. The barriers to entry are less than they would be if these women were having to arrange childcare, drive, and meet for hours (including pre- and post-circle visiting). Additionally, it can be easier to practice sharing the realness, rawness, and messiness of your life with women from all around the world than from your local community. We aren't having our needs for touch and in-person warmth met (until we meet in person and can hardly stop hugging and loving on one another at our retreats!), but we are meeting our needs for contemplative conversation, story untangling and retelling, empathy, feeling heard and being seen, and feeling treasured by other soulful, seeking women. This allows us to feel better resourced and supported in general, in order to then go out into our local communities and meet the needs that we can't meet virtually.

In other words, we've got to get away from perfectly met needs as the goal and move toward meeting them in as many creative and courageous ways as we can. In order to overturn the system, we have to use the resources we *do* have to our advantage.

Mentorship + Intergenerational Connections

Time and again, when supporting clients in creating their best lives, I hear the same sentiment expressed in different ways: "I just wish I had a wise elder to guide me through this difficult season. If only I had someone to support my process, to help me see what's most important, and reassure me that everything is going to be okay."

Our hunger for mentorship is deep and widespread for good reason. For eons, community mentors were our primary means of support, guidance, reassurance, teaching, skill development, and empowerment. Confidence was fostered, wisdom and traditions passed down, and a felt sense of belonging was cultivated naturally when a less experienced community member spent time with someone who'd been around a while.

Today, due to many factors—including the myth of independence, the breakdown of interdependence within local communities, and a general lack of reverence for our elders—most of us feel more or less on our own as we face life's many challenges. We have more decisions to make than ever before, yet little guidance to help us make those decisions well. Sure, we can now Google our way through tough times and daunting decisions, but information gathering is not the same thing as wisdom acquisition. We may collectively know more than ever before, but Googling can't begin to compare with the warmth, comfort, anecdotes, passion, intuitive guidance, presence, compassion, empathy, consciousness shaping, and caring of a seasoned human.

We've also lost touch as a culture with the importance of connecting with people of different ages. Our early years in school—where most of us were grouped according to age—trained us to seek connections with people in similar life stages as our own, but the truth is that our lives can be greatly enriched by the connections we cultivate with teenagers, 20-somethings, and 70-somethings, alike. One of my closest friends is 69. She adds a unique richness to my life that I value beyond measure, and I know she'd say the same about me at age 42. My late-20-something cousins are some of my favorite people in the world to spend time with, given their optimistic, wholehearted, playful spirits. I have become quite close with a handful of my teenage daughters' friends, who know they can come to me with their concerns, struggles, and dreams, alike, and who inspire and motivate me with their energy and idealism.

Thankfully, mentorship is something that each of us can choose to reclaim in our lives. It may be a dying art, but its necessity is rooted deep within us. Likewise, intergenerational connections are available to any and all of us who are willing to get creative and think outside the box when it comes to the ways we relate and what we need to feel whole and supported. There is as much to be gained from a tube float down the river with a bunch of 20-somethings from our workplace as there is a monthly breakfast date with our 85-year-old neighbor. Inviting a neighbor kid with a troubled homelife to play at our house on the regular is as legitimate a way to have a positive impact on our community as volunteering at a local shelter for abused women.

Who do you admire in your community? Who among your more elderly neighbors might you invite to walk with you regularly or take dinner to on occasion? Is there an entrepreneur in your town whom you admire and could buy lunch for or offer to hire as a coach or consultant? Might you exchange goods or services with someone from your church or your kids' school? The internet makes it easier to find organizations and like-minded people, but it has its limitations, particularly when it comes to connecting with older folks (who aren't always online or particularly internet savvy). We must be willing to interact outside our comfort zones in order to make unique connections that inspire and grow us.

Here are a few points to help you expand your thinking around mentorship and intergenerational connection building:

- *Good mentors won't always be older than you.* Many factors contribute to a person's ability and willingness to be a mentor, including work and life experience, hardships, resilience, free time, current stressors, sources of inspiration, and financial stability. Age often brings maturity and wisdom, but so can unique life experiences, healing from trauma, and years dedicated to a singular craft or passion.
- *Good potential mentors don't always see their own value.* Many elders within our culture don't recognize their own worth, in part because our culture doesn't honor them or their wisdom. Your ideal mentor may be surprised that you see strengths and gifts in them worth gleaning from. Pointing out these gifts can be as much a gift to them as their imparting of wisdom is to you.
- *Good mentorship may cost you.* Sometimes, getting the support, training, and healing experiences we need means hiring teachers, coaches, therapists, or those skilled in the healing arts. Though investing money in such a way can feel frivolous or unnecessary, it's often money well spent and sometimes life-changing.
- *Connection comes first.* Rather than asking a stranger to mentor you or be your friend, start by building a connection through smiles and casual conversation with that person. Let

the connection grow over time. It can feel overwhelming to be approached for mentorship by a stranger.

- *Trade and barter for goods and services.* This is a great way to keep exchanges feeling equitable and mutually beneficial. Again, get creative. Bone broth for mandolin lessons? Perennial cuttings for internet assistance? I'd say yes to both of those exchanges if I were asked.

- *Support groups, workout classes, and sports teams can be ready-made communities.* One of my favorite mentors ever is a woman I met at an Al-Anon meeting. I've also met mentors and dear friends of all ages through peer coaching groups, Spanish/English language exchanges, La Leche League, a pickup soccer league, a rowing team, dance classes, and writing groups.

- *Websites and apps can be great places to start.* Meetup.com is an awesome place to find people grouped around common interests. Likewise, the dating app concept now exists to help you find like-minded friends. Some of these include Tinder Social, Bumble BFF, MeetMyDog (for dog lovers), Atleto (for finding workout partners), Momco, and Hello Mamas. This may feel unnatural at first, but it's a great example of ways we can use technology to our social advantage (and it can be quite effective).

Patience, courage, and creativity will take you far when it comes to creating your tribe. Remember, you're not the only one looking to create more and better connections. People everywhere are starved for community and authentic interaction. Do it for you. Do it for them. Do it for us all.

Chapter 15

REWRITING YOUR CONTRACT

Another world is not only possible, she is on her way.
On a quiet day, I can hear her breathing.

—Arundhati Roy

Here's the short of it, dear mother:
We can't afford to pretend to love motherhood. Not this version of it.

The version that has us raising kids alone in homes disconnected from one another, immersed in a culture of judgment and perfectionism, under the illusion that we're the ones who can't get our acts together.

The version that's breeding anxiety and depression at epidemic levels.

The version that has us starved for realness and intimacy and glorifying the denial of our needs and desires.

The version that has us editing the imperfections from our lives in a desperate attempt to feel that we belong somewhere, anywhere.

The version that's keeping us so overwhelmed and exhausted that we aren't able to tap into our fullest potential and be the changemakers and cultural healers we're meant to be.

If being a "good mother" means sacrificing our needs and desires, we are not only modeling the denial of our needs to our children. *We are also perpetuating the narrative that mothers are less worthy of thriving than others.*

If being a "good mother" means doing as much as we can without having to ask for help, we are not only enduring isolation under the watchful eye of our kids. *We are also perpetuating the narrative that mothers aren't worthy of support.*

If being a "good mother" means never taking breaks, we are not only exhausting ourselves and limiting our access to joy. *We are perpetuating the narrative that mothers are less worthy of nourishment and rest.*

Modern-day motherhood is not just stressful and overwhelming. It's giving birth to a whole new form of oppression comprised of cultural norms and narratives that set up mothers to feel disempowered and inadequate and make our thriving extremely difficult. Pretending everything's fine and taking it upon ourselves to endure our circumstances (the unrealistic expectations, the unrelenting stressors, and our deeply unmet needs) for the sake of our children's well-being and the preservation of our identity as "good mothers," is noble and sometimes necessary, but it's also perpetuating these new forms of oppression. By "keeping up" with status quo motherhood and allowing our dysfunctional culture to determine the quality of our lives, we're unwittingly becoming complicit in our own suffering and disempowerment.

The good news is that women have never before had so much collective voice, privilege, or authority to change our circumstances and better our lives. By deconstructing our stories, developing compassion for and kindness toward ourselves, becoming dedicated stewards of our soul fires, and connecting authentically, bravely, and creatively with one another like our lives depend on it (because, ultimately, they do) we can begin to release ourselves from the spells of inadequacy, unworthiness, shame, codependency, and fear that we've inherited from the mothers and grandmothers before us. This positions us for the world-healing work we were made for.

More good news is that, whenever we're ready, each of us can choose to rewrite our maternal contracts. You and *only* you get to decide what's worthy of adding to or erasing from yours.

Life-Giving, Soul-Fueling Contracts

Several years ago, during a particularly heart-wrenching and messy season of my life, I discovered a narrative buried so deeply, and hidden so well within me, that it could almost have been mistaken for an actual *part* of me. The story went something like this:

> The mark of a devoted, wholehearted, spiritual being is the willingness and ability to endure hardship and emotional suffering for the sake of others. Truly evolved spiritual beings are unaffected by their surroundings because they are able to transmute any and all negative energies into love and light and peace. My purpose is to endure pain and longing toward my personal growth and eventual transcendence.

The unearthing of this story within brought me to my knees. Pried open and rubbed raw by my life circumstances at the time, my heart felt like it might burst from the pain of this unexpected discovery, of this lifelong unconscious agreement. I suddenly understood that I had spent the bulk of my adult life attracting and even *creating* hardship so that I'd always be surrounded by opportunities to prove my strength and dedication as a spiritual being.

In that moment of heart-wrenched fury, I wrote out my old agreement—the shitty first draft of my soul contract—and beneath it, scribbled the following, wildly, soul fire raging:

THIS ISN'T MY STORY ANY LONGER. I REFUSE TO LIVE THE REST OF MY DAYS UNDER THIS DISTORTED, SELF-ABUSIVE SENSE OF PURPOSE.

Sobbing my way through the excruciating realization of decades of self-abandonment and abuse, the freshly-liberated truth of my existence flowed through me and onto my paper:

My purpose in life is to shine the light of my soul as brightly and courageously as possible and to orchestrate my life in such a way that supports, encourages, and inspires my soul's shining.

No more fighting against those who perpetually dampen my coals. No more settling for kindling on *my* fire while constantly chopping logs for others. And no more expending the bulk of my precious time and energy simply trying to be okay under circumstances I'm not suited for.

"I'm a maple tree planted on a sandy beach," I realized in that moment. "No freaking wonder I'm not thriving."

Getting clear on my soul and life's purpose has made all the difference in my mothering journey. I no longer feel bound to *any* contract, if I'm honest, but if I had to draw one up, it might read like this:

I, Beth Berry, agree to shine the light of my soul as brightly and courageously as possible for the rest of my days. I agree to orchestrate my life in such a way that supports my shining and encourages my thriving mind, body, and spirit. I recognize that my mothering journey will continue to offer me opportunities to evolve and expand my ability to love people well, and I accept these opportunities, so long as they don't require self-abuse or neglect. I also recognize that my girls will continue to change and grow in unique ways that I cannot control, and I commit to growing and healing, myself, in order to be able to guide them, love them, and even let them go, with wisdom, tenderness, trust, and a lighthearted spirit. I will do my best to model healthy, inspired living, and a joy, fun, purpose, and love-filled life, extending grace and compassion to myself with as much heartfelt adoration as I do to my children. I will make choices that grow my self-trust, I will help them grow to trust and guide themselves, and I will trust The Sacred Mother and all her beautiful blessings to hold and nurture them during the moments and seasons when I cannot.

Surprisingly, this contract not only feels lighter, but it also feels way more powerful. Who knew those two things could exist *together*?

My new contract feels rooted in who I know myself to be at the core, my purpose as a wholehearted person (not merely a mother), trust, surrender, curiosity, and my messy, all-in love of life rather than utopia-seeking out fear and misguided idealism.

Your contract (should you choose to create one consciously rather than living from the unconscious, unexamined one each of us starts the journey with) is sacred. It can act as a blueprint, a roadmap, and/ or a filter for the hard decisions you make and commitments you take on. It can serve to strengthen your intuition, your "absolutely not," and your "hell yes!" It can even help you untangle yourself from familial, religious, and cultural narratives that have the greatest choke hold on you, such as those that one of my clients described as her "moral obligation to stay disempowered and hate myself." A good contract can serve as a spiritual guide, gently steering you back to the truth of your worthiness, importance, and true belonging over and over and over again.

Your spiritual contract (for motherhood, womanhood, and *self-hood*) can help to counterbalance the inevitable challenges inherent to *waking up*.

The Challenges of Being Awake

While untangling ourselves from personal and cultural narratives may sound simple, the vines and tendrils we're caught up in often have the tightest hold on the most vulnerable parts of us. Many stories we've always assumed were true are wrapped up in our worthiness, lovability, capabilities, failures, perceived inadequacies, traumas, and the pain we've caused others. This makes untangling them a process best done with patience, tenderness, and within reach of at least one trusted someone whom we can lean on when the false sense of security we've depended on for years begins to crumble.

There's no doubt about it: growth can be painful. But the pain of growth and healing feels different than the pain of self-abandonment. Both can hurt like hell, but one feels like soul-starvation and the other like hard-won liberation.

Telling truer stories—about the world and especially ourselves within it—is a kind, courageous act of rebellion. It's kind because truth-filled stories ultimately create less confusion and pain for everyone; it's courageous, because it means sacrificing the old, familiar, default stories in order to make room for truer, status quo-challenging stories to emerge. Braving truer stories also tends to raise the defenses of those who prefer the comfort of the way things have always been, who live in denial and complacency, or who profit from the illusions they perpetuate.

As we wake up, those who aren't ready to awaken, often become uncomfortable. This means that we must become increasingly okay with other people's discomfort in order to become more fully ourselves.

Your growth (and the choices you make that support your growth) doesn't have to make sense to those around you. In fact, in order to expand into the fullness and wholeness of who we really are, we will eventually and inevitably upset the status quo. We will upset, disappoint, concern, aggravate, and/or enrage some of the people we've historically been invested in pleasing, proving ourselves to, and/or seeking validation from. It can make a world of difference to have others on their own growth journeys alongside you during these times, to remind you of your strength and the truth of your worthiness.

Some of the most essential growth I've experienced in my journey so far happened when I let go of what my parents might think, what my husband (at the time) might think, and even what my best friends thought of me. Each of these choices to continue following *my* truth was incredibly uncomfortable, even terrifying at times. And each has been essential to cultivating the felt sense of wholeness I now cherish more than anything else in my life.

If this idea feels daunting (it sure did to me), start small.

Skip with your kids through the produce aisle (they'll likely never forget it). Make a list of all the things you'll do once you cultivate the courage. Meditate on a park bench and breathe through the discomfort of what people might be thinking. Disrupt your defaults and get a little uncomfortable, on purpose.

Then, as you slowly build strength, play a little bigger.

Say "no" to volunteer opportunities at your kids' school that you've historically felt obligated to say "yes" to and begin to notice what happens in your body. Take that job that lights you up inside but pays a little less or confuses your folks. Plan a night or weekend away from your family. Give some energy to that creative or entrepreneurial desire that no one else seems to understand or appreciate (yet). Every time we override the voice that says, "but what will _____ think?" or "but _____ might think I'm _____," we are slowly building tolerance for the type of discomfort we *need* in order to feel the way we long to feel.

I don't know about you, but *whole* and *free* and *wild* and *empowered* and *soulfully connected* are at the top of that list for me.

Mothers Rising

Women are remembering. Mothers are waking up, the world over. Never before have we had so much potential for connection alongside so much freedom. This is an incredibly powerful combination once we wake up to our interdependence and put soulful, healing connection at the top of our priority lists. Just think of the world we can create once women and mothers grow to trust and adore rather than judging and fearing one another!

The world I'm here to cocreate is sister-heavy and mama-led. It's full of restoration and tender trusting and abundant safe-feeling spaces for growing and healing and holding. It's rich with cultural narratives and social structures that honor women, revere mothers, and support us in our power.

The world I'm here to help heal into existence is one that recognizes the traumas and lies and manipulation throughout our personal and collective history and refuses to perpetuate these narratives by responding from unhealed, untended woundedness.

The future I'm here to help birth is one that slows us down, encourages self-reflection, and listens for wisdom rather than reacting from fear, scarcity, or pain.

If there's one message I hope you'll take from this book, it is this:

Until we begin to organize our lives around not only our children's worthiness but also our own, mothers will continue to bear the brunt of cultural pain and dysfunction.

Why does this matter?

Because we cannot be the changemakers we're meant to be while so heavily burdened.

Keep going, mama. Keep growing. Find yourself, then find your people. Or do it the other way around. Just don't settle. Don't ever settle for a way of life created by those who don't honor your soul and cherish your babies.

The world desperately needs you in your rightful place of power.

ACKNOWLEDGMENTS

I am deeply thankful to the following people, whose support of my seven-year book-writing journey, influence on my twenty-five years as a mother, and encouragement along my journey back to myself, have meant the world to me. I wouldn't be where or who I am today without each of you.

Sigorni—for introducing me to pure love and for being my single most influential spiritual teacher. Your strength of spirit and insistence on self-authority are qualities that I admire deeply. You have no idea how much you've shaped my life and grown my heart.

Taos—for making love feel easy and playful and for daring to shine so brightly. Your passion, courage, and wholeheartedness inspire me to live bigger and bolder. Me siento tan orgullosa de ti, mija.

Eli—for your kindred tenderheartedness, compassion, and sensitivity and for being the easiest one. ;) (Though, you don't have to be easy. In fact, I encourage you to be a pain in the ass more often. It'll serve you well in the long run, babe, I promise.)

Estella—for your fiery, feisty strength (I admire your assertiveness, even when it pushes me to my edges) and for letting me see the softness beneath it. Oh, and for your dedication to rhythm and rituals. They've comforted me as much as they have you through the years.

Hunter—for the eighteen years you supported my passions, for contributing to my freedom every other week (while fiercely loving our girls), and for being the easiest-going co-parent a mother could ask for.

Kay King (Mom)—for all the ways you nourish and nurture, for your handmade home, for your modeling of health and wellness, and for teaching me to trust my intuition. I will forever count your love for and help with Sigorni among the gifts I cherish most.

Vic King (Dad)—for modeling leadership, kindness, craftsmanship, and gentle masculinity. Thank you for encouraging me to explore the depths and for being a father figure to my girl during those dark and scary days.

Lara Carter—for loving me unconditionally and enthusiastically your entire life. I've always admired you (even when I was acting like a selfish jerk) and will forever be grateful for your generous spirit and huge heart.

Abby Crump—for modeling gentle strength, faith, and steadiness, even while you're enduring more challenges than most will ever experience.

Sherry Berry (Grandberry)—for your generous, wholehearted, playful spirit and endless love for our family. You will forever be an example to me of wholehearted authenticity, resourcefulness, optimism, and resilience.

Dennis Berry (Grandpa)—for your steadiness, consistency, love, and generosity. I'm honored to have witnessed and been touched by your lesser-known soft side.

My MotherWorthy Mamas—for sharing your stories, hearts, and lives with me and for trusting my imperfect leadership. I have endless respect for your courage and growth and endless love for our ever-deepening sisterhood.

The Revolution from Home Community—for reading and sharing my ponderings, for helping to strengthen my voice and confidence in using it, and for contributing such deep wisdom to the conversation. A special thanks to those of you who've been with me since the Mexico years. It's an honor and a privilege to have such an amazing community of changemakers bettering the world alongside me.

The Daily House Team—for helping me get out of my own way and holding my hand through the finish line.

Carly Esslinger—for being the best damn cheerleader a girlfriend could ask for. Thank you for listening wholeheartedly, for holding me tenderly through so many messy moments, for always trusting my process, and for making the madness feel so much lighter.

Anna Thornton Matos—for witnessing my messy-ass growth and being my faithful process person during my darkest days. Our phone calls were my lifeline through a thousand shit storms.

Mark Love—for recognizing and reviving dormant, neglected parts of me. Thank you for growing me as a writer, feeding my spiritual hunger, and helping me heal from religion, all the way back to God.

Amy Brennan—for your witchy wisdom, devotion to the depths, and trust in me. I'm thrilled to be making magic together.

Marti Purdy—for responding so generously to my prayer for a wise elder and becoming such a cherished friend. I adore our fireside sharing, pondering, and bullshit dismantling. You inspire me to live bigger and adventure more often.

Christi McGuire—for your meticulous editing, stellar communication, and generous affirmations.

Jennifer Daigle—for creating such a safe, supportive container for my growth and healing and for seeing and strengthening the healer in me.

Carson Fustes—for always encouraging my creative passions, for never judging my messy life, and for being so generous in your support of me and my family.

Luna Broesche—for your lighthearted spirit and wide-open heart and for living your life at such a consistently high vibration. I always feel lighter and loved after spending time with you.

Christy Tashjian—for inviting me to knit and initiating my journey back to myself. Your wholesome, homespun-mama nurturing warms and grounds me every time you cross my mind.

Kim Black—for raising baby girls with me, for opening your home to our family time and again, and for keeping those early years real and magical-feeling, no matter how insane or big our broods.

Jote Khalsa—for capturing the truth, beauty, and heart of motherhood, and allowing your powerful images to accompany my words.

Stephanie Camfield—For modeling wholehearted, all-in, instinctive mothering for me. Thank you for never apologizing that your home was a mess while you fed your soul outside.

Christine Nieporte—for making mothering in Mexico even more meaningful (and way more fun!).

Valeria Roldán—for brainstorming book titles with me and helping me feel less alone during my tropical dark night of the soul.

Mary Ellen Lough—For inspiring me to slow down, feel my way to the sacred, and live a more enchanted, poetic life.

Jessica Chilton—for our super soulful biz hikes and for shining your light more courageously than anyone I know.

GB Khalsa—for helping my babies into the world with such skillful, soft, sacred strength. Your example of gentle, healing leadership has impacted me more than you know.

MariMikel Penn—for your caring competence and for making my first home birth one of my sweetest memories ever.

My Inner Nine-Year-Old—for guiding me back to my most essential truths and desires and for saving me from the burden of hyper-responsibility.

My Inner Eighty-Year-Old—for reminding me of life's brevity, for encouraging my wildness, and for giving it to me straight when enough's enough.

The Woman at the Craft Store When I Was Seventeen and Nine Months Pregnant—for approaching me with genuine excitement and caring, looking me straight in the eyes, and telling me with the conviction of a prophetess that no matter what anyone thought about my situation, I was going to be an amazing mom. The ripple effect from that thirty-second connection hasn't stopped yet.

The Women and Men Who Cleared the Path Before Me—My deepest gratitude to the trailblazers, the lightbearers, the witches, the healers, the mothers, and the grandmothers now passed, particularly those who risked their lives fighting for freedom and sovereignty. I feel your loving support through sunny windows, observe it in the dance between trees, and hear it in the birdsong every day.

READY TO
DIVE DEEPER?

If you're anything like me, your hunger for growth and healing is insatiable. Perhaps you're ready to explore a new frontier by connecting with like-minded mothers and strengthening your sense of sisterhood. Or maybe you'd simply like to feel encouraged and rooted for via social media. Whatever your flavor, here are a few suggestions and resources to get you started:

Social Media
I am active on Instagram and Facebook. Find me at Revolution from Home on both, and add your voice to the conversation (#motherwhelmed).

Revolution from Home
My website, Revolution from Home (www.revolutionfromhome.com), is all about accelerating social change through the support, encouragement, and connection of awakening mothers (and mother lovers). Peruse years of blog posts, check out my latest offerings, explore my 1:1 coaching packages, and/or join a MotherWorthy circle. All open-minded beings are welcome. Make sure to subscribe so you'll be the first to know about new offerings and blog posts.

1:1 Coaching

My greatest passion is supporting women as they navigate the complex and confusing intersection of empowered womanhood, conscious motherhood, and personal growth. My favorite clients are those with hearts of changemakers, who are committed to making a difference and living vibrant lives, but who often feel overwhelmed by their responsibilities, critical of their efforts, and unsure as to how to most effectively invest their precious little spare time and energy. My role as your coach is to meet you where you're at, help you determine where you want to be headed, and offer you tools, perspectives, encouragement, and gentle guidance as you take courageous (and sometimes scary) steps into the unknown. I want to see you thriving. I also want the world to benefit from the unique light and warmth of your soul fire. Visit https://revolutionfromhome.com/one-on-one-coaching/ for all the information.

MotherWorthy

MotherWorthy is an intimate, yearlong program designed for awakening mothers who are fed up with the status quo, ready to get real, and inspired to cultivate change from the inside out. It's for mothers who refuse to settle for the isolation, perfectionism, and judgment plaguing modern-day motherhood and who are willing to get messy and courageous in the pursuit of a better way. Join us from anywhere in the world! We meet virtually three times per month, then circle up for an in-person retreat the following summer. We go deep, we hold one another's hearts, we deconstruct personal and cultural narratives, we reawaken our wildish nature, and we hold space for healing and growth, however challenging or messy it may be. I've witnessed few things sweeter in my lifetime than the sisterhood cultivated in these circles. Head to my website (https://revolutionfromhome.com/motherworthy/) for all the info.

RECOMMENDED READING

Here are a few favorites that have shaped my life and lit my path:

Personal Growth + Healing

Belonging by Toko-pa Turner

Women Who Run With the Wolves by Clarissa Pinkola Estés

Radical Acceptance by Tara Brach

Braving the Wilderness by Brené Brown

God Is for Everyone by Swami Kriynanda and inspired by Paramhansa Yogananda

Do Less by Kate Northrup

Untamed by Glennon Doyle

Big Magic by Elizabeth Gilbert

The Art of Possibility by Rosamund Stone Zander and Benjamin Zander

Wild Creative by Tami Lynn Kent

The Dance of the Dissident Daughter by Sue Monk Kidd

What to Remember When Waking (an audiobook) by David Whyte

The Untethered Soul by Michael A. Singer

Complex PTSD by Pete Walker

The Body Keeps the Score by Bessel van der Kolk, MD

If Women Rose Rooted by Sharon Blackie

Falling Upward by Richard Rohr

The Four Agreements by Don Miguel Ruiz

The Highly Sensitive Person by Elaine N. Aron, PhD

Warrior Goddess Training by HeartherAsh Amara

Sacred Contracts by Carolyn Myss

Bird by Bird by Anne Lamott

Witch by Lisa Lister

Codependent No More by Melody Beattie

Quiet by Susan Cain

White Fragility by Robin DiAngelo

The Soul of Money by Lynne Twist

Parenting

Live Love Now by Rachel Macy Stafford

The Fourth Trimester by Kimberly Ann Johnson

The Conscious Parent by Shefali Tsabary, PhD

This Is Motherhood by Jill Koziol

The Continuum Concept by Jean Liedloff

The Baby Book by William Sears, MD, and Martha Sears, RN

Last Child in the Woods by Richard Louv

Spiritual Midwifery by Ina May Gaskin

No Bad Kids by Janet Lansbury

Untangled by Lisa Damour, PhD

Relationships

How to Improve Your Marriage Without Talking About It by Patricia Love, EdD, and Steven Stosny, PhD

Mating in Captivity by Esther Perel

Conscious Uncoupling by Katherine Woodward Thomas

Psychopath Free by Jackson MacKenzie

Attached by Amir Levine, MD, and Rachel S.F. Heller, MA

Deeper Dating by Ken Page

NOTES

1. Charles Eisenstein, "Essay: In a Rhino, Everything," Charles Eisenstein, February 2016, https://charleseisenstein.org/essays/in-a-rhino-everything/.

2. Byron Katie, *Loving What Is* (New York: Harmony Books, 2002), 4.

3. Byron Katie, *A Thousand Names for Joy: Living in Harmony With the Way Things Are (New York: Harmony Books, 2007).*

4. Michael Singer, *The Untethered Soul* (Oakland, CA: New Harbinger Publications, Inc., 2007), 12.

5. Ibid., 13.

6. Mary Oliver, *Dream Work (New York: The Atlantic Monthly Press, 1986).*

7. Betty Friedan, *The Feminine Mystique* (New York: W. W. Norton & Company, Inc., 1997), 15.

8. Anne Morrow Lindbergh, *Gift from the Sea* (New York: Random House, 1978), 29.

9. Brené Brown, *Daring Greatly* (New York: Penguin Random House, 2012).

10. Marrianne Williamson, *A Woman's Worth* (New York: Random House, 1993), 10.

11. Johann Wolfgang von Goethe Quotes," Academy of Ideas, December 13, 2013, https://academyofideas.com/2013/12/goethe-quotes/.

12. Carolyn Myss, interview by Oprah Winfrey, *Super Soul Conversations*, OWNTV, June 24, 2012.

13. Dr. Margaret Paul, "If your Relationship is Failing, it's because you've Abandoned Yourself," Elephant Journal, May 22, 2012. https://www.elephantjournal.com/2012/05/if-your-relationship-is-failing-heres-why-dr-margaret-paul-2/.

14. Marianne Williamson, *A Woman's Worth* (New York: Random House, 1993), 16.

15. Ibid, 18.

16. Charles Eisenstein, *The More Beautiful World Our Hearts Know Is Possible* (Berkeley, CA: North Atlantic Books, 2013), 32.

17. Jon Young, "Episode 2.6.6: Aunties and Uncles," *512 Project,* Audio. September 9, 2017. http://512project.com/aunties-and-uncles/.

18. Brené Brown, *Braving the Wilderness: The Quest for True Belonging and the Courage to Stand Alone* (New York: Random House, 2017), 158.

ABOUT THE AUTHOR

Beth Berry is a mother, writer, entrepreneur, and whistleblower who believes that empowered, supported, and soul-led mothers are cornerstone to the healing of the world. Through her virtual MotherWorthy community, retreats in Asheville, the San Juan Islands, and Mexico, 1:1 coaching and mentoring, and her popular blog, Revolution From Home, she supports the rising and thriving of mothers who identify as changemakers. Beth has written for Mothering.com, Motherly.com, National Geographic's Green Living, and been published in Motherly's book *This Is Motherhood*, and Rachel Allan's *When Business Meets Baby*. She lives with her four daughters in the mountains of Western North Carolina.